DYLAN COBURN GRAY

Dylan Coburn Gray is a playwright based in Dublin. His sole-authored work includes *Boys and Girls* (winner of the Fishamble Best New Writing Award; nominated for the Stewart Parker Trust Award) and *Citysong* (winner of Soho Theatre's Verity Bargate Award 2017). Collaborative work with MALAPROP Theatre includes *Love+* (winner of the Spirit of Fringe Award 2015) and *Everything Not Saved* (winner of the Georganne Aldrich Heller Award 2017, the *Guardian*'s Best Shows of Edinburgh Fringe 2018). Both strands of his work play with form, and aim to challenge and delight in equal measure.

Other Titles in this Series

Mike Bartlett
ALBION
BULL
GAME
AN INTERVENTION
KING CHARLES III
SNOWFLAKE
WILD

Jez Butterworth
THE FERRYMAN
JERUSALEM
JEZ BUTTERWORTH PLAYS: ONE
MOJO
THE NIGHT HERON
PARLOUR SONG
THE RIVER
THE WINTERLING

Caryl Churchill
BLUE HEART
CHURCHILL PLAYS: THREE
CHURCHILL PLAYS: FOUR
CHURCHILL PLAYS: FIVE
CHURCHILL: SHORTS
CLOUD NINE
DING DONG THE WICKED
A DREAM PLAY *after* Strindberg
DRUNK ENOUGH TO SAY
    I LOVE YOU?
ESCAPED ALONE
FAR AWAY
HERE WE GO
HOTEL
ICECREAM
LIGHT SHINING IN
    BUCKINGHAMSHIRE
LOVE AND INFORMATION
MAD FOREST
A NUMBER
PIGS AND DOGS
SEVEN JEWISH CHILDREN
THE SKRIKER
THIS IS A CHAIR
THYESTES *after* Seneca
TRAPS

Karen Cogan
DRIP FEED & THE HALF OF IT

Fiona Doyle
ABIGAIL
COOLATULLY
DELUGE
THE STRANGE DEATH OF
    JOHN DOE

debbie tucker green
BORN BAD
DEBBIE TUCKER GREEN PLAYS: ONE
DIRTY BUTTERFLY
EAR FOR EYE
HANG
NUT
A PROFOUNDLY AFFECTIONATE,
    PASSIONATE DEVOTION TO
    SOMEONE (– *NOUN*)
RANDOM
STONING MARY
TRADE & GENERATIONS
TRUTH AND RECONCILIATION

Vicky Jones
THE ONE
TOUCH

Deirdre Kinahan
CROSSINGS
HALCYON DAYS
MOMENT
RATHMINES ROAD
SPINNING
THE UNMANAGEABLE SISTERS
    after Tremblay

Lucy Kirkwood
BEAUTY AND THE BEAST
    with Katie Mitchell
BLOODY WIMMIN
THE CHILDREN
CHIMERICA
HEDDA *after* Ibsen
IT FELT EMPTY WHEN THE
    HEART WENT AT FIRST BUT
    IT IS ALRIGHT NOW
LUCY KIRKWOOD PLAYS: ONE
NSFW
TINDERBOX

Stef Smith
GIRL IN THE MACHINE
HUMAN ANIMALS
NORA : A DOLL'S HOUSE
REMOTE
SWALLOW

Jack Thorne
2ND MAY 1997
BUNNY
BURYING YOUR BROTHER IN
    THE PAVEMENT
A CHRISTMAS CAROL *after* Dickens
HOPE
JACK THORNE PLAYS: ONE
JUNKYARD
LET THE RIGHT ONE IN
    after John Ajvide Lindqvist
MYDIDAE
THE SOLID LIFE OF SUGAR WATER
STACY & FANNY AND FAGGOT
WHEN YOU CURE ME
WOYZECK *after* Büchner

Phoebe Waller-Bridge
FLEABAG

Enda Walsh
ARLINGTON
BALLYTURK
BEDBOUND & MISTERMAN
DELIRIUM
DISCO PIGS & SUCKING DUBLIN
ENDA WALSH PLAYS: ONE
ENDA WALSH PLAYS: TWO
LAZARUS *with* David Bowie
MISTERMAN
THE NEW ELECTRIC BALLROOM
ONCE
PENELOPE
ROALD DAHL'S THE TWITS
THE SMALL THINGS
THE WALWORTH FARCE

Dylan Coburn Gray

CITYSONG
AND OTHER PLAYS

NICK HERN BOOKS

London

www.nickhernbooks.co.uk

A Nick Hern Book

Citysong and Other Plays first published in Great Britain as a paperback original in 2019 by Nick Hern Books Limited, The Glasshouse, 49a Goldhawk Road, London W12 8QP

Cover photography by Carla Rogers

Designed and typeset by Nick Hern Books, London
Printed in the UK by Mimeo Ltd, Huntingdon, Cambridgeshire PE29 6XX

A CIP catalogue record for this book is available from the British Library

ISBN 978 1 84842 850 8

Introduction

Boys and Girls opened in 2013, *Drawing Crosses on a Dusty Windowpane* was written throughout 2014 and 2015, and *Citysong* was written at the end of 2015. These three plays sum up two very important years of working out what and how and why I wanted to write. (Then MALAPROP – the collaborative outfit I make work with – came along, and everything got a lot more complicated.)

Citysong is the single play I've written so far that most embodies everything I'm about as a writer. But you can find the seeds in *Boys and Girls*. There are things in *Boys and Girls* too that I would not write now: pop-culture references that were dated the moment I wrote them down, jokes in the voices of young men that can only be so 'ironically' sexist if they require you, the audience, to sit there and listen to them. I'm still proud of it as a document of a time in young Irish adulthood. I'm still proud of it for having a kind of nerdy compassion at its heart. I still think there are worse things to aim for than stylish sincerity.

There's an arc to these three plays. It's not scale, even though the four people of *Boys and Girls* become six in *Citysong* with a detour through monologue for *Crosses*. I think the arc is me learning to be other people, and the journey is further each time. The work I love is all about truth, moments of unexpected recognition or realisation. The leap into someone else's experience that all at once takes you home. That said, I'm not mad on writing that is self-consciously #relatable, funnily enough, because I think it often has a conspiratorial subtext.

Don't we all do this?

Aren't we all like this?

Which invites the punchline to the old joke:

Who's 'we', white man?

It's sameness without difference, the leap without the chasm.

If the un-looked-for truth is what you look for, it would be stranger if your writing didn't sooner or later spiral out from the world you know best and find easiest to write. Meaning writing itself gets harder, but that's to be expected. The further you want to leap, the more of a run-up you need. Someone once said to me you get one good work out of doing what comes naturally, and from there it's all learning to be someone else. I think about that a lot. I like that a lot. The idea that the means is the end: connection, which is always a transformation, working at turning ourselves into ourselves who are new.

In art as in life. The one great task! To reach the point where performance becomes.

Dylan Coburn Gray
April 2019

Acknowledgements

Thanks to Róise and Kris and Ruth and Cian and Steve and Jen
and Sarah and Neil and Graham, Colm and Kalle and Stephen
and Erin and Linda, Robbie and Emma and Aisling, Sophie Jo
and Aoife and Ben and Jim, Brian and Mark and Áine and
Erica, Soho and Fringe and Project and ITI and Fishamble and
Culture Ireland and Dublin Youth Theatre, Madeline Boughton,
Aoife and Leah, Jasmine and Holly, Breffni and Claire and John
and Maeve and Molly, the Galvins, my mother, my father, my
sister, Carla. And a shout out to Paul. Wish you were here.

D.C.G.

CITYSONG

Citysong was co-produced by the Abbey Theatre, Dublin, and Soho Theatre, London. It was first performed at the Abbey Theatre on 25 May 2019 and transferred to Soho Theatre on 12 June 2019, with the following cast:

Amy Conroy
Bláithín Mac Gabhann
Clare McKenna
Dan Monaghan
Daryl McCormack
Jade Jordan

Director	Caitríona McLaughlin
Set and Costume Design	Sarah Bacon
Lighting Design	Paul Keogan
Composer and Sound Design	Adrienne Quartly
Movement Director	Sue Mythen
Voice Director	Andrea Ainsworth
Associate Sound Designer	Jennifer O'Malley

VOICES

VOICE
KATE
ROB
BRIGID
FRANK
MICHAEL
FIONN
RADIO
FARE 1–4
TAXIDAD
DRIVER 1–4
TAXIMAM
RIDER 1–2
TAXIKID
DOCTOR
BIRD 1–4
INDAD 1–4
OUTDAD 1–2
ROLL-CALL
YETUNDE
3B 1–4
NEIGHBOUR 1–4
FRIEND
SOUND DOCTOR
SHIT DOCTOR
GREAT-GRANDMA
CROSSWORD
IRISH NURSE
IAN
LOUISE
BRONAGH
CHRISSY
BUSINESS PRICK 1–4
LUSH 1–4

SWORDS NEIGHBOUR 1–4
MS BUTLER
ÁINE
BEN
SAM
MS BELTON
MS RUANE
MR O'DONOGHUE
PRIYA
INTERNET
NIAMH
AMNESTY 1–4
PARTY ANIMAL 1–4
CONCERNED PARENT 1–4
ROUGH SLEEPER 1–4
GABRIEL
JUDE THE GIRL
MUTTERER 1–4
SEÁN
STEPHEN
LAD 1–4
MATCHMAKER
DANCER 1–4

This text went to press before the end of rehearsals and so may differ slightly from the play as performed.

Performance Notes

An em dash (–) at the end of a line means you prepare the next line. No punctuation at the end of a line means the moment keeps going out of our sight.

There are a lot of words. There is a lot of imagery. If you – the performer – try to enjoy all of it, you will run out of feelings. If they – the audience – try to get all of it, they will run out of brain. Probably the approach to text should embrace this fact. I'm not saying piss through it, but it can be fast. I'm not saying be casual or flippant, but what I am saying is that it works best when the logic is cumulative. Some thoughts you pass through and some you arrive at. The engine of the text is how well you feel you're doing at getting the audience to understand. Not well, look harder for the right thought to offer them; well, enjoy the moment of shared understanding.

If a line is convoluted you know it's convoluted. There is a quality Steve Marmion generously calls The Irish Twinkle, which I would call Embracing The Fact You're A Wanker. It's self-aware but sincere. It's good panto! Commentary without ridicule.

There are rhymes and rhythms, but there's not a lot of end rhyme or coupleting. I encourage you to look for patterns that give you momentum. Sound A's recurrence begins the thought containing Sounds B and C's recurrences which leads inevitably to the thought beginning with Sound D's recurrence...

The audience is always there.

Some of the jokes are in working-class Dublin accents; ideally, the audience should never think the Dublin accents are the joke.

Because there are so many characters, most of the time the performer's age/gender/race/whathaveyou will be 'wrong'.

It's probably best not to sweat those things too much in the first place, but not in the way where not sweating it means everyone in the cast is a hot young white man.

ZERO

VOICE. It is night and here is the city, sleeping.

Riversplit and seakissed and roadrunneled and concrete brick stone steel and glass formed and typeset.

Look: the spire's a spindle or axis and while it's not vinyl the city is a record of all that has happened to us, is happening, or will. It spins as the world does and a godlike needle could read its spaces, how it bumps and juts and dimples and cavities, as pages or notes in the book or the symphony of us.

It is a legible palm, a singable psalm, ringable changes, irreducible word of the language that speaks us like Genesis or crucible whose heat both begins and then ends us.

So let's begin with an ending.

Night has lightened until it isn't, and day breaks into wholeness.

Like an egg cracked into a cakebowl and cakedom, or a wave into licks of foam on rock, or the heart of a roaming dad who yellowsignedly and oh-so-resignedly taxis through the less but still blackness.

He and the moon are waxers, lyrical and big respectively, and they wane and wain as well. The nightly, monthly and silvery moon to the horizon and an eyelashlike slivereen of its milklike, fullfat, self.

The stubbly, the weary, the double and bleary-visioned man not a shrinker but a carrier: he rubs his eyes hard as chastisement for failing him and wains in the sense – or guise – of a chariot.

Each night he's on nights he slaloms from outstretched palms into suburbs and estates where his radio awakens –

RADIO (*incoherent noises*).

VOICE. and cracklingly beckons him back into town for some short-haul transit. Like tonight, when he stopped for the hailing hands of George's Street –

FARE 1. to North Strand?

VOICE. The Five Lamps –

FARE 2. to The Ivy House?

VOICE. Gardiner –

FARE 3. to Liffey street?

VOICE. and Eden Quay –

FARE 4. to my house, please?

TAXIDAD. Which is where?

VOICE. He says, gruff, though he quite likes these oneshots, mirrorlooking at these not-much-more-than-ten-minute-or-a-fiver fares and inferring their life affairs from their from, their to, their demeanour. Is it a date or a breakup, a catchup with the once-close-now-once-a-year faces?

He can afford to waste time on them, tonight at least, he's hit a hundred already. It's no banquet or feast but in faminetimes it's hungersauced to deliciousness.

And he's been cruising for a while now, he's exhausted and he's fished out this patch of the pond, so it's time to head home.

He doesn't mind the driving, but he's never been exactly eye to eye with the other drivers. Lovely blokes, but the rankbanter betimes can be very anti-everything. With all of the complaints like –

DRIVER 1. He fuckin' dropped his chicken fillet roll

DRIVER 2. He dropped his fuckin' kebab

DRIVER 3. She was a grown fuckin' woman and she pissed in the fuckin' cab.

DRIVER 4 (*noises of disapproval*).

VOICE. And then there's the –

DRIVER 1. Fuckin', part-time drivers

DRIVER 2. Fuckin', not a sniff of them until five or the clubs close and then they're out like an army

DRIVER 3. Fuckin', sittin' on the rank like a rash but half as charming

DRIVER 4 (*noises of approval*).

VOICE. But all of that's nothing on the acid loathing saved for –

DRIVER 1. Fuckin', double-jobbers

DRIVER 2. Fuckin', bored teachers

DRIVER 3. Fuckin', bored firemen wanting cash for their lovely holliers.

DRIVER 4. BASTARDS.

VOICE. Not his buzz, he understands, but he's managing, and like he always says –

TAXIDAD. Can't complain, it could be worse.

VOICE. And his wife, who's a nurse, and who wants – but refuses – to curse at him shoots back –

TAXIMAM. That's a load of – dogbusiness.

VOICE. He's on his way to her now.

Headed in from Ringsend, where he's just dropped his last fare, headed North as the Eastlight scoops, like icecream, itself into the stillness of the still dark West. Following his homenose, he homegoes thinking –

TAXIDAD. That one went South quickly enough, like.

VOICE. It was a city-centre pick-up. Two people, thirties, a blazerless dress-shirt and a black and backless dress means –

TAXIDAD. Professionals, so my expert guess is Clontarf, Glasnevin, or somewhere in the Deep South. We'll see now.

RIDER 1. Cambridge Road, Ringsend?

TAXIDAD. No bother.

VOICE. He says, and –

TAXIDAD. Close enough.

VOICE. He thinks.

It's well past four o' clock, meaning –

TAXIDAD. Lock-in rather than clubs, for this lot anyway.

VOICE. Or then again maybe it was clubs, he's given both pause and a shock by their backseat conduct.

Like Central Bank teenagers more so than bankers, with their intertwined torsos and too-graphic noises like –

RIDER 1 (*violent kissing*). Oh my god

RIDER 2 (*violent kissing*). Oh my god

RIDER 1 (*violent kissing*). Fiona

RIDER 2 (*violent kissing*). John

VOICE. An unwanted flash of flesh in the rearview and she gasps, chokingly, says –

RIDER 2 (*violent kissing*). JOHN

RIDER 1 (*violent kissing*). FIONA

TAXIDAD. Folks, is here okay?

VOICE. He says, and they break off their kissing and oh-yessing for just long enough to say yes and pile out. The man's hand flies from wallet to the twenty ten and fiver-taking driver's, then alights – not lightly at all, but stonkingly – more horny swan honkingly than spare as a sparrowly – on her arse as they gigglingly foreplay their way up the courtyard of the building. Is it his? Is it hers? Who knows?

TAXIDAD. Enjoy.

VOICE. He says, as he reverses out the driveway.

TAXIDAD. Foreplay? More like FIVEPLAY.

VOICE. He tells his own face on the dashboard ID. It's old enough that he's young enough that he can't see himself as himself in it.

TAXIDAD. My neck was never that long but.

VOICE. It was but.

TAXIDAD. I'm squinting but.

TAXIKID You still do but.

VOICE. His daughter sometimes interjects, on those good nights when he's allowed to collect her from pints with her mates. It's one of their things, like his sing-song but sincere question

TAXIDAD. So are you locked?

TAXIKID. Nah.

VOICE. She says, normally, or not-so-normally –

TAXIKID. A bit yeah, but only a bit but.

VOICE. Or just the once –

TAXIKID. Hi, yeah, it was a

did you have a

good night it's really warm isn't it?

can I turn on the window?

lovely

can I turn on the radio?

I meant the radio

VOICE. That time, he remembers, she fell asleep on the way home and he was himself again, his long-necked and narrow-eyed photoself, who used to carry his child sleeping from the backseat to her bed undisturbed.

She is taller than he is now, and his back's fucked so that time he just pulled up at the kerb outside the house. She didn't wake so he roused her with a shake on the shoulder and a –

TAXIDAD. Get to bed, y'dipso

VOICE. rather than the cheek-kiss that he and she did and didn't wish for. Or so he thinks. He's reserved, he's always left it to her to determine when they touch. But she's at least as much like him as the wife, so maybe she's thinking the same thing of him.

He goes North to where – right now – she's asleep like then; where he'll be sleeping when she's waking and when he's waking whence she'll be missing.

As frustratingly as a falling domino kissing the next domino that trembles but doesn't fall. But where dominos kiss commonly it's seldom that she kisses him if she kisses him at all. But as he says himself –

TAXIDAD. Can't complain, could be worse.

ONE

VOICE. Let's leave him, there and then, as the sun swells
pregnantly from segment of a mandarin to half of a Jaffa
Cake, at that moment when John and Fiona have taken off to
take off their clothing.

Let's move four and nine miles and months in space and time
without leaving now, as they make love in an apartment, to
a hospital that throbs like a heart despite the hour.

Let's look instead, in this beginning instant, to this place in the
centre, this place of infant's first world-entries with placentas
like parachutes, where the dawn chorus shrills and blinds as
the sun, over and past outside's smokers and the blinds, like
a coldhanded doctor pokes the first fingers of greeting.

Who are the birds who sing here? They're not, save
vernacularly, they're women, they're pregnant, they're
wrecked and they're spectacularly pissed off with everything.

This is not motherhood meek and mild but wild animals and
viscera. High-definition and in the glistening hues of post-
lion, wide-open, xylophone-ribbed zebras, but this is an
extremity much extremer than that of those latter half of the
alphabet letters.

What good if the doctor's saying –

DOCTOR. That's good, we've got four centimetres!

VOICE. Because –

BIRD 1. THAT'S FUCKING NOTHING

VOICE. Or –

DOCTOR. Push!

VOICE. Because –

BIRD 2. I AM FUCKING PUSHING.

VOICE. Or –

DOCTOR. You've still to deliver the placenta!

VOICE. Because –

BIRD 3. WHY DON'T *YOU* FUCKING DELIVER THE PLACENTA.

VOICE. The prayer and naysayers alike are saying prayers in their sixth hour of their second day of need or desperation, making requests like –

BIRD 1. Just don't let me poo

BIRD 2. Just don't let me die

BIRD 3. Just let it be over soon

BIRD 4 (*screaming*).

BIRD 1. Just don't let me poo

BIRD 2. Just let the baby live and not not be able to breathe because she's umbilically tangled or strangled

BIRD 3. Just don't let me need a procedure with scalpels or to be given a huge fucking spinal needle

BIRD 4 (*screaming*).

BIRD 1. Just don't let me poo

BIRD 2. Just let it be done

BIRD 3. Just let the fucking baby come.

BIRD 4. JUST DON'T LET MY VAGINA RIP AND BECOME ONE WITH MY BUM.

VOICE. New men and old men are new dads alike, the former pom-pom-lessly cheerleading witnesses, the latter pompously or nervously or disinterestedly distant.

The new men are there with their sweaty hair and facedly swearing partners. They can't carrry their carrier's burden for them but they can coax them from exhaustion and back into motion with their voices choking on their burgeoning emotions in loving words like –

INDAD 1. You're doing great!

BIRD 1. FUCK YOU

INDAD 2. Just push!

BIRD 2. YOU CAN FUCK OFF

INDAD 3. Nearly there!

BIRD 3. FUCK YOU

INDAD 4. Squeeze my hand!

BIRD 4. FUCK YOU YOU MOTHERFUCKER YOU DID THIS TO ME.

VOICE. And the old men – regardless of age – are outsidedly timebiding, only arguably hiding but one-hundred-per-cent absent. They smoke with white knuckles until the pub over the road opens, but one-hundred-proof absinthe couldn't stop them from thinking about all the gore and wrackedness that's happening without them, so they chit-chat distractedly but more and more often just lapse into silence.

OUTDAD 1 (*pause*). It's probably quite tense in there.

OUTDAD 2. Oh no doubt.

VOICE. Look, here.

As the sun clears the horizon as roundly as the crown of a purple white and greasily shining baby, this woman is handed hers and he's breathing as easily as she isn't, as calm after his first grizzle as a stormless teacup and he and eggshell porcelain are equally frail.

She holds him and she traces his wrinkles like braille and for her at least it balances, the alms-less-ness of labouring with her palm now cradling her tiny pink Yorick, the balm of this night's morrow's daylight with that endless burning dark.

This is her son and her son's vernal equinox, with his sleekly blackly vernixly slicked-back thick black locks of hair that she smooths, so so carefully and so so calmly, from his perfect face as scrunched as imperfect origami.

He's healthy, he's alive, got four limbs and four sets of five on the end of them.

KATE. And thank fuck for that

VOICE. She breathes.

Her name is Kate, and her partner who's waiting for a squeeze of the baby by the bedside is Rob. This is their first kid in their late and early thirties respectively, unmarried eight years in and still not expecting to be, living in sin their parents' peers if not their parents would have called it, despaired of, tutted at, or policed, but these days who cares, really?

They're both teachers, like her father, which is a respectable profession at least, and Rob looks out the window to the streaky bacon East and thinks

ROB. The alarm went off an hour ago and no one was there to snooze it, no one toasted toast or ground grinds and around this time we'd cruise down the motorway to school, early enough to beat the rush and have a staffroom cup of tea, but we didn't today and someone else will have to call the roll for 3B and deal with all of the –

ROLL-CALL. Yetunde Mulcahy?

3B1. Yetunde's absent she's pregnant

YETUNDE. Fuck off I'm not absent or pregnant but

3B1. Ah but you're pregnant but

YETUNDE. Ah but fuck off but

VOICE. And how much better is it being here, now, holding his son for the first time, even if he's shit scared and thinking –

ROB. Just don't stop breathing and we'll be fine. How are you?

VOICE. He asks her, and she's got so many answers –

KATE. I feel like a cored apple or an ironing board with a face-down iron burning a hole in it or a chased-down and wolfsavaged deer or a dropped and cracked beer glass or a chipped sink or an iceskaters'-iceskatesedly lacerated icerink or snapped icecream wafer or a mousetrap full of brokenbacked mice or a holepunched piece of paper or floorfallen piece of meat you'd feed a stray cat or cat that's been hit by a truck and tiretrackedly flattened to the point of bursting and the worst bit's its visible guts on the tarmac, that's how I am.

VOICE. But she just says –

KATE. Tired.

VOICE. And takes the baby back, and dozes like her mother does right this instant, alone in her home in Donnycarney by the church she's never gone to.

Kate naps like her mother did in the 1980s, having just had her, her fourth of four otherwise all male babies –

BRIGID. Thank god all still living

VOICE. And all born if not in this room then at least in this building.

Her name is Brigid, for the saint, her husband Frank, for his father, but he's two years gone, or late, or departed, and never again will he be coming home early.

He still stares out of mantelpiece pictures that span the wall and nearly half a century, from their black-and-white wedding in his borrowed suit finery, the both of them as unlined as their clothing and smiling as widely as they were able, to their crumpled colourlessness in later colour, their hair as white as once it was sable.

She doesn't know about Kate's baby, not yet.

But if she did, in this moment as the church throws its silhouette butterfly-net-like in the window and onto their photographed faces, the dozens of the between two and five of them in different sizes, times, and places, she'd be thinking about their births –

BRIGID. Michael, then two years, Stephen, then three years, Seán, then five years later Kate.

VOICE. Ten years of pregnancies and as fearful or more so at the end as at the start, once again gowned and hobbling in the arterial throb and hum of the hospital and once again thrummed by contractions like an on-the-verge-of-snapping guitar string, waiting on Kate to come and so once again praying –

BRIGID. Just let it not hurt too much and let it be a girl because I've had enough of boys, sons and their father, and don't let me die from poison in my blood or endless bleeding like poor Mrs Whelan, god rest her, or even be invalided like poor Mrs Cahill who – slow as a Roman slave in *Spartacus* in shackles – shuffles in her slip-on shoes – because she can't face bending for laces – to Black's shop and back every day for the messages in a daily Gethsemane's-worth of agony, world without end, from here on earth into eternity. They say she says she saw he had a saw and even the nurse screamed.

Just let me live, healthy, let the baby live, healthy, not like the Nolans who went in the two of them and came out the two of them and probably the two of them never even got to see him.

VOICE. She can and could imagine what that was like, somewhat at least, having lost. Before Kate and after the boys she'd been pregnant, till on the cusp of crossing the cusp of first and second trimesters, she bled, not much, but more than enough to make her worry and hurry to the doctors in the hopes of being mistaken, who offered her nothing but shaken heads and shrugged avowals of helplessness, that there was no one and nothing could help her with this, these hours of pain and labour on a day not just weeks but months too soon.

And driving home from the emergency room Frank had nothing to say but –

FRANK. It'll be alright love.

VOICE. For all he said it often, that was all he ever said, first or last thing in the morning or evening or their bed.

FRANK. It'll be alright love.

VOICE. But it wasn't and it wasn't because he was, and she was furious because he wasn't, raging that he could act so normally in the face of such an abnormal enormity.

BRIGID. We're both still speaking English but we no longer share a language. I am anguished that I am feeling anguished when you don't seem to be, and I'm angry and I'm angry that I'm angry and you're not. So stop eating your workday breakfast or your weekend lunch, stop telling me about work today or stop playing with your sons that I gave birth to, stop eating your everyday dinner and acknowledge that this hurts you, unless it doesn't and if it doesn't then what in god's name is wrong with you, stop laughing at *Hall's Pictorial Weekly*, you prick, stop laughing, stop humming that Sinatra tune you're always humming, how can you want to hum?

VOICE. She knew too about the workings of whispering gossip, that post any pregnancy or mishap if a mother seemed distant or drawn her neighbours would trade titbit for tatbit of her trauma in voyeuristic barter and comment annoyingly knowingly with heads nodding and brows bobbing –

NEIGHBOUR 1. She's a martyr to her nerves, the poor woman, a martyr.

NEIGHBOUR 2. Did you hear she?

NEIGHBOUR 3. And you know he?

NEIGHBOUR 4. He didn't!

NEIGHBOUR 1. He did.

NEIGHBOUR 2. Sacred Heart.

NEIGHBOUR 3. Where does he get off.

NEIGHBOUR 4. Sher where would you even start.

NEIGHBOUR 1. Sher look.

NEIGHBOUR 2. This is it.

NEIGHBOUR 3. I know.

NEIGHBOUR 4. And did you hear about the Mahers?

VOICE. But she didn't feel 'nervous', in any state of hysteria, uterine fear, endometrial trembling or ovarian dolour, not like any kind of Demeter lacking any stolen Persephone.

If anything Frank had a case of testeria, a gonad madness or scrotal psychosis, but either way a lack of a wound that was one. Or so it seemed to her then.

BRIGID. Never again.

VOICE. She promised, though will she or nill she the pill was still pre-scription only, even for the not-so-happily wedlocked. So supportive friends said things like –

FRIEND. I know a nice doctor and if you go to him he'll ask you –

SOUND DOCTOR. And are you 'irregular'?

FRIEND. And then you say yes, you're 'irregular', and he'll sort you!

But make sure it's the nice one, because the other one just says things like –

SHIT DOCTOR. Try to live as brother and sister with your husband.

FRIEND. Or if your kidneys are bandy then they'll sort you in Holles Street, are your kidneys bandy?

BRIGID. No

FRIEND. Then just say you're 'irregular'.

VOICE. But she never even had to because it happened on its own.

The way it had always gone, before and after they were married, was Frank would say –

FRANK. Would you like a kiss love?

VOICE. And she would say –

BRIGID. I would actually!

VOICE. And then he'd give her more than that, by a more than large margin, that's unless the day'd been so long that trading sex for rest seemed like a bargain, and then she'd say –

BRIGID. I feel a bit sick love, mightn't be wise, you might get it.

VOICE. Which was also what she said to him when she was on her period, and she never knew if he ever knew that it didn't always mean that, because his response was invariably a –

FRANK. Right so, I hope you feel better tomorrow.

VOICE. Overnight, after, he just stopped asking, and she never asked him if that was from anger, sorrow, guilt, grief. But as long as the long time she was angry it was a relief, and in those days her days went –

BRIGID. Breakfast for Frank and the boys and me, then I stay here with Stephen and Seán, and Frank and Michael leave to go to school as pupil and teacher as well as father and son, and I do whatever there is to be done around the house which normally sees us to one o'clock and Jesus what do I do now other than make lunch and clean it up and make dinner and clean it up, I could call in to Anne if I wanted to and wanted the bother of dragging the boys out of *Wanderly Wagon* and into the buggie, which I don't.

I could listen to or look at something or read if I wanted, but I'm haunted by the emptiness of everything with an ending which is everything. The present is dead and the future is its ghost.

I do both the crosswords, simplex and crosaire, but that's just the guts of an hour at most.

VOICE. In those days if someone asked what made her happiest she might have answered with something like –

BRIGID. Sometimes we go to the Killester to see *Superman* or *The Muppets* or *Watership Down* which scared them because they kept killing the rabbits, and that's always quite nice because I don't have to do anything.

Or in the summer maybe Dollyer if it's a nice day, swaying the whole way out there on a brand-new not-blue-but-orange double-decker with my hand holding the overhead pole that's slick with the sweat of strangers, and me boldly barelegged

under the sundress I only ever wear to the beach, with two
sons clinging to my two legs like ships' masts, then one tired
son sat on one foot and then a tired son sat on each.

And at the beach I buy ninety-nines from the Mr Whippy
van, and it won't be one minute till one of them drops theirs
in the sand, and then I'll give him mine, and look at the
water, as blue and as white as my mother's mother of god
statue that frightened the life out of me when I was tiny, and
I listen to the sea sing as it slumps in, tongues the rocks, and
slouches out muttering, listen to gulls grouching in tinwhistle
voices and I look at all that blueness, and have a sense in that
moment of the world's momentary brand-newness as though
nothing's ever happened, to me or to anyone, or everything
has happened and it's finally over but either way it's not that
I suddenly feel amazing, I don't, but I don't feel terrible.

VOICE. Each of those moments ended as time ticked onward,
not cruelly but unstoppably, and her life resumed where it
had briefly left off.

But that's what she might have said if asked, only no one
ever asked her.

Things were never fixed, reversed, nor did they cease to hurt
her, but time makes most things lighter if not blunter.

Meaning ultimately it was her said to him –

BRIGID. Would you like a kiss love?

VOICE. And he said –

FRANK. I would actually.

VOICE. And then she gave him more than that, by a more than
large margin.

So soon after when she started to balloon with Kate she was
scared but not angry, not with him, not with herself, and with
the boys all in school by then Kate was hers and no one
else's, leaving her hours and hours for gratitude. Not in any
crampless cradlingarm happy holding, not in any wellrested
golden lassitude, but at the least with babe abreast asleep
exhaustedly thinking –

BRIGID. I'm going to spoil you rotten to thank you just for being.

VOICE. Later on, having a girl was different to boys, no doubt, but different things were different than she had thought would be different.

With the boys she was used to saying –

BRIGID. Don't do that, it's not nice, don't be coarse, love.

VOICE. When what she meant was –

BRIGID. Stop trying to fit your whole hand inside your foreskin.

VOICE. She thought her little female angel would be different, kempt where they were un-, shevelled where they were dis-, as decorous as that coarse chorus of lads weren't, god bless them. So imagine her horror at having to say –

BRIGID. Love, you mustn't ever do that, not even in the house

VOICE. When what she meant was –

BRIGID. Stop rubbing your vagina all over the arm of the couch.

VOICE. That's what she would remember, if she knew, but she doesn't, so she doesn't.

She's only now waking, and dressing her aching but still capable body in ten-year-old clothes that billow where once they gripped, the black and sail-like silk shirt and the slacks she cinches with entire inches tighter freshly bored belt-holes on the ship's-prow proudly jutting promontories of her hips.

Where once she was fairycakes and fish and chips and rasher cooked in cookeen rounded, even when she wasn't pregnant to the point of feeling like a heffagalumphing and lumpen elephant, these days she's far more in common with any kite than any zeppelin.

Her mother always called her a –

GREAT-GRANDMA. Fine solid girl

VOICE. Which she hated but wouldn't now she finally isn't.

She goes downstairs, slowly, and pours Shredded Wheat, which she hates less than other cereals but still hates – but still eats – because she's not allowed cook now.

The cooker and floor are dialless and rugless respectively, since she burned her face and arm badly a year and copper change ago. They're replaced in the new arrangement by a microwave she hates as much or more than she hates cereal.

BRIGID. Too many buttons.

VOICE. She always says.

And the mornings she briefly forgets that things are like this she asks herself –

BRIGID. Who labelled the drawers? Why label the toaster? Who's cleared the floors and where are my rugs now?

VOICE. Struck by looking at her home of half a century and not seeing anything she's come to expect to see.

She goes to the door and she picks up the paper, delivered on Frank's subscription but which the children now pay for.

She's still got the kettle so she clicks it on, picks up her pencil –

BRIGID. Simplex then crosaire.

VOICE. And the simplex is as simple as it ever is, but she comes a cropper on the crosaire as she seldom does, or seldom used to, on –

CROSSWORD. Twelve across, seven letters, second and seventh letters are an A and an E, lace with una corda to make absences –

BRIGID. I haven't a notion what that could be.

VOICE. But it isn't just that she doesn't know, it's that she's staring at 'absences' because –

BRIGID. I don't know if I know that word or if I have ever known it or even what it means.

VOICE. Which scares her, so she stops, which leaves her cross she's leaving uncrossed Ts and Is undotted, because in her eyes if you can't finish then there's no reason you should bother and underneath that she's bothered that this is happening more often.

BRIGID. I can still do the simplex.

VOICE. She tells herself, which would still be cold if it were comfort but it isn't even comfort.

She always took pride in her daily pair of completions, simple and cryptic, which she would subtly leave in view as an autolaudatory diptych and privately sneer at mere simplex-solvers, but now she thinks –

BRIGID. Just don't let there come a day when I can't do either of them.

[*If your production finds the unanswered crossword clue distracting/annoying, you can use one of the two following optional moments. Moment one begins here, following the line directly above:*

VOICE. And –

BRIGID. I'll show Kate

VOICE. Her word-nerd daughter, her mother's mind's treason's revenger, relied upon to know that both the answer and the reason Brigid can't remember it is –

KATE. Lacunae, plural, gaps or emptinesses.

VOICE. Occupied with forgetting she's forgetting Kate's occupied, Brigid doesn't hear the key in the door which means Ian is here now.

Optional moment one ends here. If you're not using it, just go straight from Brigid's line ending 'I can't do either of them' to the line below:]

VOICE. She doesn't hear the key in the door which means Ian is here now.

Ian is Filipino and his name is Ian so –

IRISH NURSE. Howye, Filip-Ian-o!

VOICE. Is what the Irish nurses say to him because –

IRISH NURSE. It's funny because it's your name and you're from the Philippines!

IAN. That's funny!

VOICE. He always says, but –

IAN. That's not funny.

VOICE. Is what he means.

IAN. And I've a good sense of humour.

VOICE. Which he shows, along with kindness and patience, to his patients, like Brigid, for whom he's family when family can't be.

[*Optional moment two, if you don't want the clue to dangle, begins here, following the line directly above. Note: this moment requires a sufficiently literal blocking/staging that* IAN *can look over* BRIGID*'s shoulder at an actual newspaper. It goes:*

IAN. Lacunae.

BRIGID. Sorry?

IAN. The clue, lacunae, plural, emptinesses!

Optional moment two ends here. If you're not using it, just go straight from the line ending 'when family can't be' to the line below:]

IAN. Are you ready for our pilgrimage Brigid?

BRIGID. What?

IAN (*in a self-congratulatory breath that leaves no room for response*). It's a trip to the shops it's not a pilgrimage don't mind me what am I like Brigid are you ready to go to the shops is what I mean don't mind me!

VOICE. He could and probably should go on his own but she won't let him. If she writes him a list she always forgets something and when she forgets she's too ashamed to say anything and –

BRIGID. I'm not one to sit by and let someone else do everything.

VOICE. Step by sensibly shoed step they progress past hundred-year-old bungalows, in the crisply chilly lettucelight of midmorning to the Centra where Black's newsagents once was.

He offers her his arm, and –

IAN. People will think I'm your boyfriend Brigid!

VOICE. He says, and –

BRIGID. Ah stop

VOICE. She replies, because she's pleased and shamed that it's a joke and that she likes it. He's a nice-looking man but young enough to be her son's son almost.

He handles her money and he carries both bags back, for all she offers to take one, unbags and cupboards or presses without correction the few bits or messages, finally asks her –

IAN. Cup of tea?

BRIGID. If you don't mind

VOICE. And –

IAN Boiled egg?

BRIGID. If you don't mind

VOICE. She answers, uncomfortable, always the one who did for so being done for makes her feel done for.

But Ian is graceful in her defeat, blankets her in chat as he first cooks then re-neatens the kitchen where she's sitting in oblique sun and thought, until her attention is caught by the phone ringing at midday, which Ian answers and hands her so she can say –

BRIGID. Hello?

ROB. Hiya Brigid, how are you, it's Rob?

BRIGID. Yeah?

ROB. Your daughter Kate's fella?

BRIGID. Yeah?

ROB. I'm just ringing to tell ya that the little one's arrived and so far he's doing fine, his head's a little squashed but that's normal, apparently, a baby's head is always soft, and his eyes are cataract-free and the only hole that's in his mouth is the hole that's supposed to be. His heart works, his lungs work, his spine's like a palm tree and his palms have two creases and his hips move easily and his urethra's in the right place, thankfully, I didn't know it mightn't be but apparently it mightn't be and as soon as he does a black sticky poo we're all clear but you probably don't want to know that, I didn't want to know that, anyway, he's fine, it's deadly.

BRIGID. Lovely!

ROB. Yeah, and it looks like we'll be home tonight if you want to come meet him? I'll pick you up and bring you down and drop you back afterward?

BRIGID. Lovely!

VOICE. She says again, because the tinniness of the phone means she's getting at best one word in three, and lovely's a safe answer to anything he might have asked her.

Rob sits on the other end with his sleeping child and sleeping Kate. He thinks –

ROB. By the time you've known us as long as we've known each other you'll be eight, and you'll have changed completely. Your eyes'll've darkened, your skull'll've hardened, your teeth'll be grown in only to start to fall out. Whereas we'll be the same, give or take, more or less, just like we're the same, give or take, as when we met.

VOICE. Rob arrived to an all-girls school in the middle of his twenties, which meant the girls had plenty more than plenty to say about him, like –

3B1. He's alright-looking like

3B2. Easily a seven like

3B3. A six though

3B4. A seven if he was dressed better and didn't sweat through his shirts like that it's mental like it's like he's got taps in his armpits like

3B1. Would you though?

3B2. I would though

3B3. I wouldn't though

3B4. You should fucking be so fucking lucky you fucking fussy cow

VOICE. And plenty to say to him like –

3B1. Sir what's your type though?

ROB. That's nothing to do with oxbow lakes or erosion.

3B2. Is it blonde though sir?

3B3. Curvy sir?

3B4. Have you ever been in love sir?

3B1. Are you in love now sir?

3B2. Do you love 'em and leave 'em sir?

3B3. Sneak out while they're sleeping sir?

3B4. Do you fancy Yetunde sir?

YETUNDE. Fuck off Joyce

3B4. You fuck off Yetunde you're pregnant

YETUNDE. I'M NOT PREGNANT Y'POXY BITCH

ROB. Who can tell me if podzol soil is nutrient-poor or nutrient-rich?

VOICE. The staffroom then was staffed by respectable teachers, mostly women and all Catholic and all coffee-break preachers on state of the nation, immigration, abortion legislation and sundry such not-really-up-for-debate debatables.

Like Louise, who used to say things like –

LOUISE. I'm not saying they all steal, but you can't say they don't steal.

ALL (*noises of agreement*).

VOICE. Or Bronagh, who used to say things like –

BRONAGH. If abortion was legal then I wouldn't be here!

ALL (*noises of agreement*).

VOICE. Or Chrissy who used to say things like –

CHRISSY. And he was black but what was his name only Michael, just like he was normal!

ALL (*noises of amazement*).

VOICE. What got Rob and Kate talking was seeing the other not talking.

The teachers had a shed for the smokers to smoke in, for the gasping for a gasp to gasp in, and Rob remembers meeting her there, sat on a broken lawnmower with cobwebs in her hair, and how Kate then asked him –

KATE. Do you have a smoke?

ROB. I do yeah.

Pause.

KATE. Can I have one?

ROB. I suppose yeah.

KATE. That's such a fucking dad joke.

ROB. 'I don't know, can you?' (*Go to the bathroom.*)

KATE. 'Time you got a watch!' (*What time is it?*)

ROB. 'Then stop doing it!' (*It hurts when I do this.*)

KATE 'You don't look like one!'

Pause.

ROB. Don't know that one.

KATE. 'I feel like an icecream'?

ROB. Do you?

KATE No, that's the –

ROB. I know it is, I was just being a prick.

VOICE. Two years till they moved in together off Pearse Street, a tiny one-bedroom wherein they weathered the boom and crash on their uncivilly sliced in crisis civil servants' salaries, not that that stopped all of the –

BUSINESS PRICK 1. Well for some.

BUSINESS PRICK 2. Not for all of us.

BUSINESS PRICK 3. Three good reasons, I suppose.

BUSINESS PRICK 4. JUNE JULY AND AUGUST

ALL (*self-congratulatory noises*).

VOICE. Five years till they bought a house, post the post-tiger summit prices' plummet, in Swords, where they live now.

Marriage occurred to them, but neither of them's fussed on it. They would have if their parents had felt that they must do but Rob's aren't around, and even when both of Kate's were they were both super-sound about it.

FRANK. As long as you're happy love.

VOICE. Her dad had said, and –

BRIGID. Once you love each other love.

VOICE. Was her ma's take on the issue. And Michael, her oldest brother's was –

MICHAEL. Imagine there's a sauce you can put on your dinner, and if it's something you already like to eat then it tastes as sweet as a mortal sin or as savoury as gravy or both at the same time, it's as delicious as any dish has ever been basically, but if it's something you don't like then it tastes shit and kills you so why take the risk, yeah? You wouldn't, yeah? Logic, yeah?

That's marriage. Don't get married. When things are good you don't need to be and when things are bad you don't want to be, marriage will leave you let-down, fucked-up and empty as a modern-day mass on a rainy day. Don't get married, I'm telling you.

VOICE. Michael is divorced.

Her other brothers escaped to London and Australia, and Michael had wanted to but ultimately failed to, in part because of the son and split he does and doesn't regret. Fionn's now fourteen, which is strange for Michael because his son now looks like he used to, and sometimes still thinks he does till a mirror or a window disabuses him in passing, every facet of every glass a potential cruelty.

MICHAEL. I thought that I saw my dad on Grafton Street and I was glad for all of half a fucking second till I remembered and realised it wasn't it was me looking like him.

VOICE. He came home and told his girlfriend recently.

MICHAEL. When did all my hair go?

VOICE. he asked her and

RACHEL. You've still got lots of hair though

VOICE. She told him kindly if not exactly honestly.

Rob and Kate have just started to feel that feeling, since leaving town and their twenties, the onset of entropy in their bodies and surroundings: everything's down and never-backward motion, haggarding or effacing both faces and places however loathed or beloved.

Once their mornings were peopled by last night's lushes lounging louchely at bus stops lacking buses, antiheroic or Heathcliffily watching the stoic suits who transLiffeyly rushed to crunch numbers, occasionally hailed with a –

LUSH 1. Got the time?

LUSH 2. The day?

LUSH 3. The date?

LUSH 4. The year?

VOICE. But these days it's all casual nods to neighbours in businesswear, a hurry and a four-wheel drive.

SWORDS NEIGHBOUR 1 (*spoken with an ingressive breath*). Hi.

SWORDS NEIGHBOUR 2 (*spoken with an ingressive breath*). Hi.

SWORDS NEIGHBOUR 3 (*spoken with an ingressive breath*). Hi.

SWORDS NEIGHBOUR 4 (*spoken with an ingressive breath*). Hi.

VOICE. But town is no longer their town anyway.

KATE. Our cafe's closed now

ROB. and they changed our pub's name to market to stag dos

KATE. and the whole of Dolier Street is one big Starbucks

ROB. The whole street?

KATE. The whole street yeah

VOICE. But all of that pales for them next to the paling and darkening, the filling out and collapsing, of their bodies as they lapse towards more relaxed contours.

ROB. When did my hair grey?

KATE. When did my teeth yellow?

ROB. When did these lines around my eyes suddenly line up like potential criminals?

KATE. I know they're not that visible but it still freaks me out because I know that they're going to be, these sparrows'-for-now but eventually crow's feet.

ROB. When did these lines either side of my nose get so painfully obvious like the ones the students paint on to play schoolplay grandparents?

KATE. When did the skin on my arm start to slacken into an incipient bingo wing that doesn't yet flap but eventually will? Who allowed this?

VOICE. Their oldest online photos, from their earliest days together, have gathered a certain air of wistful distance.

KATE. I've got terrible hair and you're really thin.

ROB. I've got a terrible moustache and even worse skin but you look the same to me, basically

VOICE. And Kate, who was six months and ten kilos into pregnancy when he said that, said to him –

KATE. You're lovely, but that's a load of absolute hoop.

VOICE. So ultimately they concluded –

ROB. It's strange to me that I look strange to me

KATE. Because I don't remember changing.

VOICE. Just like Brigid, in her living room, indifferently watching one of the one thousand channels Michael pays for for her, glances aside and catches the eyes of her younger and current selves, her here and now reflection super-imposed over the posing photo-figures ranked on her shelves.

BRIGID. There I am and there I am but I don't think I look like me, I still think I look like that, twenty-four and fancy-free but that was a long time ago and it shouldn't still surprise me but it does, each and every time as much as the first. Someday it might not, when my hair's spent longer being white than ever it was dark but not yet.

VOICE. That photo of her wedding – from when her whole life was one third of her whole life now – doesn't seem that long ago, or not any more long ago than other things seemed then.

She was ten years working like but younger than Kate when she married, and school seemed as distant as Hong Kong or Buenos Aires on the classroom globe had been.

She remembered then after ten years what she remembers now after sixty: not much but reading, writing, 'rithmetic and knuckle or wrist smacks with rulers from Ms Butler, who peppered her English with Irish and her Irish with English –

MS BUTLER. An bhfuil all of you go léir ag éisteacht go gcarefully to me?

VOICE. And she remembers how she and the forty-four girls in the class finished for good at fourteen. Brigid herself off to a job in a launderette her friend Áine got for her, tentative and scared but with her mother in her head saying –

GREAT-GRANDMA. When your brothers are older you can go back to a technical.

VOICE. Only that never happened, for her or the most part, because by the time they'd grown up they were grown-up and engaged.

Nor did she need Áine's warning that –

ÁINE. If you're on your own you mustn't get in the lift with him or the other one, either of them, you know what men are like, and you know what they say about Jew men.

BRIGID. I actually don't.

ÁINE. You're lucky then.

VOICE. She always found Mr Ben and Mr Sam – as they were called – to be paragons, in hat-tipping passing as she dealt with the nylon and rayon, pinstripes, pinafores and linen of posh men and yet posher women, or in conversation and their smoke-filled office for the office of Friday paytime.

Their worst misdemeanour was telling the boring story of how something nearly happened to them in the reserves in the 'Emergency' Ireland had instead of a world war.

BEN. It sounded very much like it was perhaps smugglers

SAM. Very much

BEN. But it was Proinseas!

SAM. Proinseas!

BEN. Proinseas with his funny name

SAM. So funny

BEN. Which was I think good definitely

SAM. Definitely

BEN. Phew!

SAM. Phew!

VOICE. Which she could always handle, easily if not delightedly, nodding politely till handed her weekly nearly two pounds, one for her mother and household messages, though she'd often do the shop herself in Dunnes on the way home to save time, because her mother never forgave the world the shocking travesty of walkaround supermarkets.

GREAT-GRANDMA. It was nicer with the lovely counter and I can never find the stupid parsnips.

VOICE. Brigid got to keep six-two and sixes for herself, an unimaginable wealth to be hoarded dragonlike, the bullion basis of her few days of seaside ebullience and nights of excitement at dances or the pictures.

And though he's never seen a shilling, Fionn, her grandson, the age now she then was, dreams of that much purchase, so much more than the weekly tenner he stretches to cover the covert cider his plans for later depend on. Though for now he's stuck at school, three classes in, has already dealt with

Ms Belton who puts blanks to be filled in in the middles of words she's already started –

MS BELTON. And now we need to find the lowest common denomi...?

Denomi...?

Denomi...?

ALL....nator.

VOICE. And Ms Ruane, who teaches SPHE from experience

MS RUANE. Me and Gavin were so relieved then when I finally got my period, you wouldn't believe it, we thought our lives were over, and that's why you use condoms –

VOICE. And Mr O'Donoghue who isn't – but wants to be – in the IRA.

MR O'DONOGHUE. People today might not take Sinn Féin seriously but as you can see we – I mean they've a noble history of opposing the inherently dysfunctional operations of British colonialism at moments when the governments of the Saorstát lacked the balls to, the courage, sorry, not the balls, I didn't say that.

VOICE. Fionn's phone clamours in his pocket as he unlocks a locker full of mould-speckled sandwiches, saying there's a message from his dad saying –

MICHAEL. Meet your new cousin!

VOICE. With a photo of this fuzzy-haired purple-red blob of playdough and he thinks

FIONN. They had a baby.

They had sex.

They're old.

Ew.

VOICE. But then he's young enough that he can't imagine exactly what he's imagining, having never even so much as tried to kiss anyone.

He's known the mechanics for a long time: his mammy, who he lives with, explained after Priya Kearney – whose doctor parents believe in correct language for anatomy – told him in third class –

PRIYA. Sex is when a man shoots semen on a woman's egg and then it turns into a baby in her uterus.

VOICE. Which left him thinking –

FIONN But how does he shoot it? What is semen? Women have eggs? Where do they keep them?

VOICE. So later and tentatively he asked the internet for –

FIONN Sex videos?

VOICE. And the internet told him –

INTERNET. Barely legal teen gets enormous creampie! First-time teen on casting couch! Amateur teen screams while choked and assfucked! Petite blonde teen goes ass to mouth! Asian teen blowjob, Latina teen blowbang, Czech teen wrecked by gangbang anal, girl from Ivy League college in library threesome with painful double penetration!

FIONN. That was really scary and I still don't understand.

VOICE. He thought, with his mind newly opened by those squeamishly-closed-after-two-minutes pages, and –

FIONN. I don't think I ever ever want to be a teenager.

VOICE. Only now he is, and it isn't like it seemed then online, now that he thinks he wouldn't mind if it was. And back then his mother must have seen because she sat him down and told him –

NIAMH. It's natural to be curious but there's bad things out there

I don't mean to scare you but

Sex in real life is not

Sex is nice. Not nice.

Lovely? Not lovely.

Sex, sex is, sex is like… the best hug.

Deadly? Maybe.

VOICE. And the practical factuals followed, not like when Brigid tried to enlighten Kate, at the age of nine, after seeing Nicolas Cage and Cher sharing a *Moonstruck* moment.

BRIGID. When a man and a woman love each other they get into bed.

That's not all, there's more to it.

Pause.

They're different

men and women

not completely just certain bits

and they fit like a jigsaw or an

I don't know

a key and a keyhole.

There you go now.

VOICE. But she herself got neither bird nor bee, let alone a treefull or buzzing hive of them, just her mother's brusque –

GREAT-GRANDMA. When you're married you wear a nightie.

Not pyjamas, a nightie.

VOICE. She wasn't yet a great-grandmother when she said that, or ever when she was alive, and if anything it's in spite of her advice that she became one.

But so it goes anyway, regardless of our half or full-arsed or hearted entreaties, our shrugs or utmosts, time slogs on and makes hosts of every individual, fathers of sons and grandmothers of mothers, aunts of sisters and uncles of brothers, lovers of lovers of virgins and widowers of widows' lovers.

We multiply each other, not our bodies but our functions, unfold into roles like uncharted continents, travelling daughterward or husbandwise or widdertwins, becoming through the compass of kin and no matter whether we wouldn't or would.

And today's baby opens his eyes and inherited blood like a map, a book, or the heavens.

TWO

VOICE. There are dead hours here while it rains, as it always does, heavy enough to navy pale denim and puddle so that everything is wavily double-imaged underfoot, a billionangled mangled reflection, a studiously liquidly Cubist study in perspective set to the millionmutter of guttergush, the rushing whoosh of carwheels rilling, the percussion or trilling of concrete and tarmac lacquered with a liquid pelt pelted until it sings, puckering and puckering in concentric rings in Ouroborosy palimpsest.

Shop doorways are sudden forests of shoppers caught short and skin-soaked, while bright-yellow Amnesty workers Alexandrine Pharoslike stoically anorak onward –

AMNESTY 1. Hi, how are you doing!

AMNESTY 2. Have you got a minute!

AMNESTY 3. Howdy partner!

AMNESTY 4. Horrible day isn't it

I won't keep you long so but

okay bye

VOICE. Taxis are sudden celebrities, hailed by the previously dryly indifferent. Our pal from before is not among them, he's asleep still.

The light is a neitherthing that could be dawning night or dusking day, a crepuscular betweenness.

The city has stopped, or slowed at least, as people postpone what can be till tomorrow.

Rob and Kate are still with their son, who's still sleeping.

Fionn is in his mother's, pointedly not doing his weekend homework.

Michael is with Brigid, as he always is on this day, and if it
were a nice one they might go for a drive, to a park or to the
seafront, and walk as they did when she was taller than he was.

But it isn't, so they don't, but will again some other day.

They drink tea with the telly on as rain tattoos the window
like a free-jazz drummer or a freely doodling artist.
Raindrops rivulet and rivulets pathway, in split-second forms
like how musical notes chord and the chords then hymn,
theme, fanfare or melody.

The rain passes until it's past, and the city can start again.

And this here is the important part: people may stop when it
rains but their clocks don't, with their hands like restless
semaphore-sayers, that clasp and then part again in noon and
midnight prayers, and their peaceless motion in ceaseless
devotion bespeaks or betokens no granting of mercy to us.

Time ticks onward, not cruelly, but unstoppably.

Time – both like and unlike the rain – passes and is endless.

So let's us continue.

ONE AGAIN

VOICE. Let's end with a beginning.

Day has darkened until it isn't, knelled by the bells of
churches it kneels and peels off its shell or armour like a
hardboiled squire or egg and is nighted. The sudden dark is
cut by the bonfire-bright but heatless orange of sodium
streetlamps, coldly fluorescing, cone-ing luminous teepees
into the octopus-inkishly tinctured streets.

Fionn is here in the centre of the city, a recent freedom his
ma Niamh has ceded to him, unlike the two cans of Devils
Bit he's got in him, both secret and illicitly.

She said to him –

NIAMH. I suppose that you're old enough and you have to start
eventually.

VOICE. But this new sundering can't help but leave her
wondering how he's doing, for all that she tells herself –

NIAMH. I remember being fourteen and wanting to go to parties

VOICE. But part of why she's scared is remembering what
happened at them.

PARTY ANIMAL 1. David's after friggin' the box off Shauna in
the shed!

PARTY ANIMAL 2. Gas!

PARTY ANIMAL 3. And Martin Shankey spat at a vigilante
and then they took him away so we think he's dead…

PARTY ANIMAL 4. Oops

VOICE. Fionn's been to birthday or GAA club discos, but this
one's in town and a nightclub that most nights save this one's
for grown-ups, and she knows this because she asked the
internet

NIAMH. This night like, is it safe like?

VOICE. And the internet told her –

CONCERNED PARENT 1. There's drinking and smoking

CONCERNED PARENT 2. There's smoking and fighting

CONCERNED PARENT 3. My Yasmin says they were not just sitting but LYING on the couches

CONCERNED PARENT 4. How is it allowed like did you ever hear the like of it like where are their parents

CONCERNED PARENT 1. One word: bingefingering

CONCERNED PARENT 2. Three words: knickers in airvents

CONCERNED PARENT 3. And my Garth says a girl drank three naggins and nearly died there!

CONCERNED PARENT 4. And I saw a foreign national driver in a taxi with three girls getting into the back in their short skirts!

Pause.

I'm not accusing him of anything

but if he were to choose to do something awful then

I mean it just goes to show or makes you

that's all I'm saying

VOICE. None of which – by any stretch or in any way – reassured her.

But she holds it in and holds to a thought which she chants like a god or buddhaless prayer or mantra –

NIAMH. Just let him be safe, and happy, and safe, and let him do as he said he'd do and not be dead and come home not dead by eleven.

VOICE. When he'll once again be her pumpkin or some kind of shortchanged cut-short Cinderello, but not just yet.

This is a night of firsts for him first.

First time begged to with the rote-as-prayer urgency of roughsleepers who've pegged him as a potential listener.

ROUGH SLEEPER 1. Excuse me

ROUGH SLEEPER 2. Sorry to bother you

ROUGH SLEEPER 3. Bus ticket

ROUGH SLEEPER 4. Hostel

ROUGH SLEEPER 1. Nineteen

ROUGH SLEEPER 2. First night

ROUGH SLEEPER 3. Three months

ROUGH SLEEPER 4. Ten years

VOICE. First time walking past sleeping bags and tents,
    chrysalises in stasis, blood flesh and bone encysted in plastic,
    unrecognised by the numbly comfortable city as self.

    Not Fionn's first time drinking but his first time paying for it,
    pouring his saved pocket money into the pool that Gabriel
    Ojelade – who had to shave for his confirmation – uses to
    buy for mates or anyone else suitably desperate.

    First time here and witness to the madness of it, the madly
    glad abandon of those with hands up and voices hoarsened
    from lyricscreaming, whose dark bodies in darkness are the
    shadowy arrows of forces graphed in flesh, in the feverish
    press of stomachs and backs and sweatrivered limbs and
    flashingly split secondly lit slivers of faces.

    It terrifies him, the bassy gutpunch of kickdrums and blaring
    idiot treble that mix to make a deafening fuckoff
    charivarevelry which veers between charts and classics older
    than the dancers dancing to them, the latter with their
    heartfelt synth sounds the latter-day charts insincerely ape,
    coupled with the couples with mouths hungrily agape,
    anemone-tongues waving and interweaving in welcome and
    hands as peregrine as peregrine falcons, it's too much for
    him to take in much less handle.

    Fionn had hoped he'd look good in his one good button-
    down grey shirt that hides his sweat patches and soft belly,
    his long hair slicked back with a half-pot of posh gel that he
    secretly bought because his mam doesn't like gel.

NIAMH. The heads on them, the neck, the state, the HACK,
    like old shit boybands or horror-movie rats.

VOICE. She always says, but Fionn hopes others like the look
    even if she doesn't.

But somewhere inside him, alongside the cider, there's this
    horrible feeling, like he is the one thing without any place here.

He feels like a halfthing, a doughboy, a scared child.

His friends have been absorbed into the middle of the
    dancing so he hangs out on the periphery, knowing he's
    failing but nonetheless trying to be at ease if not in truth then
    appearance at least.

He can't stop thinking –

FIONN. I don't want to be here, this was a mistake

VOICE. And then Gabriel appears like his biblical namesake
    and speaks unto him in ciderladen thundervoice –

GABRIEL. WHY AREN'T YOU DANCING JUST DANCE
    MAN WHY AREN'T YOU DANCING

VOICE. And he wants to but can't say –

FIONN. I can't

VOICE. Or –

FIONN. I don't know how

VOICE. So instead he says –

FIONN. In a minute!

VOICE. And escapes to the smoking area, the rough-tongued
    facelick and minty lungprick of night air and braziers, where
    his panic subsides – but doesn't die – amongst smokers too
    intent on smoking to sneer at him.

For fear of looking weird he writes on his phone – so that it
    looks like he's texting a best mate who's absent or some such –

FIONN. I'm useless, I'm fat and I'm awkward and I can't talk
    to girls or stand this music, I'm stupid with stupid clothes
    and a stupid hairdo and I hate that I don't know what to do

and that they do, when did everyone learn this and why can't I learn it, when did everyone turn this corner and why can't I turn it, what is it I'm lacking or missing that means it's so easy for some people to dance or kiss people when I can't, why can't I, and why don't I want to?

I'm ugly, I must be.

VOICE. Writing it out doesn't help, exactly, but it makes sense of his panic and fact of his fancy, like it's not something he's not doing but something he can't not be.

So he's calm if not happy when someone says –

JUDE THE GIRL. Hi Fionn!

VOICE. And –

FIONN. Hi Jude!

VOICE. He says back, because Jude's in his school.

And female, which he knew but slightly less than coolly and newly registers with an up-and-down perusal that takes in her yellow skirt and croptop, the which – unbeknownst to him – her older sister chose for her, dressed as such to the nines if not quite the present moment. He's never seen her bellybutton before or the rest of her this dressed up and he thinks she looks tip-top and so he says –

FIONN. You look

deadly?

JUDE THE GIRL. Like broccoli?

FIONN. What?

JUDE THE GIRL. Sorry, there was this ad when we were kids and the kid in the ad said –

FIONN. 'Broccoli, deadly!' I remember now, sorry, I'm stupid.

JUDE THE GIRL. No you're not.

VOICE. Jude's not someone he really knows but she's easy to talk to, one-on-one, meaning when she says –

JUDE THE GIRL. FUCK I fucking love this song, do you want to go and dance?

VOICE. It suddenly seems the easiest thing to say back is –

FIONN. Yeah me too

Yeah okay!

VOICE. And follow her breathlessly as she warps through the weft and wefts through the warp of the carpet of partiers, slowly but surely becoming a part of it themselves.

She bounces her head so he does and points at shit like she does, and then there's a bit of the song that goes something like

JUDE THE GIRL. YOU AND ME!

VOICE. which she sings along to, right into his face, and her breath races across his like some kind of small animal, warm and alive on him, and he suddenly wonders – but doesn't dare – but wonders nonetheless, but doesn't know if she wants him to or if he's supposed to so he hedges his bets and says –

FIONN. WHAT?

VOICE. She leans in even closer and he doesn't know if she does it or if he does but it's happening.

They kiss.

Not neatly.

But both timelessly and all-too-briefly, a lapseless moment of ecstatic stasis that collapses when they remember that they need to keep breathing, because time ticks onward, not cruelly but unstoppably.

He doesn't know this but the song that's playing is 'The Lovecats'.

If Kate, in the passenger seat of her car and homebound, turned on the radio and were to hear that song right now she'd remember feeling as tiny and hollow as Fionn just did, for all that she had the wake of three brothers to follow into adolescence, as various in their teen tribes as in their current countries of residence.

Michael drank in Bartley Dunne's when he underagedly started to, nursing his beer and his grudge for all the barmen who refused to serve pierced ears or the blokes who were attached to them.

He was drinking there years before he caught on to the mutterings of mutterers that –

MUTTERER 1. They glue coins to the floor in there.

MUTTERER 2. They do though

MUTTERER 3. It's true but

MUTTERER 4 (*noises of agreement*).

MUTTERER 1. And I heard there's nothing on the jukebox but disco

MUTTERER 2. Them fuckin' Julians but

MUTTERER 3. Them fuckin' Sandies though

MUTTERER 4 (*noises of agreement*).

MUTTERER 1. They iron too.

MUTTERER 2. They sew and all.

MUTTERER 3. And dance with ther hips.

MUTTERER 4. Disgraceful them queers disgraceful, has it really come to this?

VOICE. Which might have made him not go if it hadn't been knocked down shortly afterwards anyway.

The year of Kate's first outing Séan and Stephen were out-and-out animals, raving ruthlessly and raising the roof of The Olympic where their parents both like and unlike them used to dance couthly. In those days they'd arrive home Rhubarb-and-Custarded into incoherence, or White or Speckled Dove lovebuzzedly trying to muster an appropriate appearance for breakfast.

She remembers Brigid asking them –

BRIGID. Are the pair of you alright like?

VOICE. And them saying –

SEÁN. Is it just me or is the light really

STEPHEN. Yeah I'm

SEÁN. Is there any because I'm

STEPHEN. Food just hungry like you know yourself the

SEÁN. Fine thanks for

STEPHEN. Bit of a headache actually.

SEÁN. Might go back to bed like

STEPHEN. Bed yeah

SEÁN/STEPHEN. Bye

VOICE. She missed that by a few years, only just old enough
for heading out at all, dressed in her skirt and jacket double-
denim best in the community centre, slightly before the
Spice Girls' complete global takeover, only just older than
'The Lovecats' was then.

She remembers the swaggering braggadocio culture of
virginal but nonetheless vulturous boys, remembers their
raucousness in the unsultry swelter, their faces leopardpelted
with mirrorball brightnesses as they screamed things like –

LAD 1. Titty?

LAD 2. Yeah

LAD 3. Box?

LAD 2. Yeah

LAD 4. Under the knickers?

LAD 2. No

LAD 1. Shit one

LAD 2. Yeah.

LAD 3. You?

LAD 4. Yeah

LAD 1. Decent?

LAD 4. Half-decent

LAD 2. Shit one

LAD 4. but in fairness a bit of an Underworld as well but in fairness

LAD 3. What?

LAD 4. 'Born Slippy'!

LADS (*self-congratulatory noises*).

VOICE. And she remembers thinking –

KATE. When did everyone learn these words and why didn't I and why are they so sick, so horrible, with all of the Twixes and boxes and Kit Kats and bits got and tits groped and I wish that I could not know but I can't not now I do.

I can't imagine – I can imagine – but I can't imagine wanting to there in front of everyone, not even kissing, does that mean there's something wrong with me? Is no one else scared? Is no one else wishing that they could be somewhere, anywhere, where this isn't happening? Am I the only one? Am I gay, or a robot, or meant to be a nun?

VOICE. She wasn't, in the end, for all she feared she might be.

And she knows she kissed someone at one of them at some point, prompted by a matchmaker who Genesis-style snaked up to her and earscreamed –

MATCHMAKER. Will you meet me friend?

VOICE. And she knows she said –

KATE. Yeah okay

VOICE. But not who they were or how it subsequently went.

She does remember her first kiss with Rob, after a work do, which ended – as they all do – in Coppers, amongst the high and well-heeled taking spills and coming croppers on the spilled-pint-and-punters'-sweat-anointed dance floor, amongst the bouncers built like hearses and the Garda-chasing teachers

and the teacher-chasing nurses, Rob and Kate's colleagues
among them with all of their

LOUISE. Look at yer man there I'd say he's a Garda now

BRONAGH. Ask if he's a Garda

CHRISSY. HELLO ARE YOU A GARDA

LOUISE. He's a Garda!

BRONAGH. A sexy Garda

CHRISSY. I love a Garda.

L&B&C (*collective noises of approval*).

VOICE. So Rob and Kate pleaded off, leaving them to their
own devices and vice of choice, the eighth Catholic
sacrament of entrapment of lawmen.

They walked down Harcourt and along the Green,
pretending not to see shining-signed taxis as they slowed for
them, and when they got to the moment of parting both of
them found they hadn't the heart to immediately.

KATE. Goodnight.

ROB. Goodnight.

KATE. Goodnight though.

ROB. Goodnight then.

KATE. And also goodnight like

ROB. Good point, goodnight so

KATE. And also goodnight like

ROB. Good point, goodnight so

KATE. And also goodnight like

ROB. Are we just going to keep doing this?

KATE. You tell me.

VOICE. She doesn't know if he or she did it but it happened then.

They kissed, and it was deadly, as in broccoli, not as in sin, for all they'd done it before with others and would go on to do it again.

Neither of their firsts but a first nonetheless, and all the better – if not the best – for being unasked for, same as the first night they later spent together.

They were meant to see a film but they were late for the start of it, and Kate forgot she'd parked her car at Rob's for just long enough to drink a few drinks and then cop when they got back –

KATE. I can't drive home

ROB. No you can't.

Pause.

KATE. A taxi?

ROB. Have you the money?

KATE. Not really.

Pause.

ROB. You could stay here?

KATE. You're sure?

ROB. Of course, but obviously you don't have to.

KATE. Obviously

ROB. Obviously

KATE. Cool.

Pause.

ROB. Are you going to?

KATE. Yeah.

ROB. Cool.

VOICE. She wondered if he wondered if she'd done it deliberately, and years later discovered he'd worried mirror-imagedly.

Both both and neither of their decisions at the same time, both excited, both shitting it, and Kate remembers – as his keys turned with metal crepitus – her inward litany of –

KATE. Let all of both of us not smell weird or manky, and don't let him be someone who thinks all women like spanking, or choking, or hairpulling, and if he likes teeth like I like teeth then let him like them used carefully.

Don't let him be into no craic porn positions and poses, let there not be loud weird or embarrassing noises, don't let him notice I've got legs like carpets, don't let him notice how ancient these knickers are and if the thing happens then let me not get sick on him and let's hope he reciprocates without throwing a fucking freaker.

VOICE. But it happened as it generally does, never ever as good or bad as either feared or hoped for.

And things have changed over time, like their bodies have, for all Rob's claim that –

ROB. I know I've gotten fatter like but my stomach's still flat if I hold it in and stand up straight and never ever sit down in front of people.

VOICE. Pleasure is always pleasure, but excitement can diminish as experience annexes innocence, and sex is one of the areas where that's felt keenest. But they've talked about how –

ROB. I think about being single but also being single is difficult and I was shit at it so on balance I'm pretty happy and not bored, are you bored?

KATE. No.

ROB. You sure?

KATE. I think so.

ROB. Deadly.

VOICE. Which has been good enough so far, at least.

And there's another type of timelessness that only comes with time, the endless homecoming of knowing someone so wholly that their soul becomes tangible in their body like a language that you've never not known.

The bilingual and languorous exchange of innermost and singular strangeness till it's strange no longer but feels like home.

And those times out of time, like all others, end, when someone says something like –

KATE. You're on my hair

VOICE. or –

ROB. I've got a cramp

VOICE. or –

KATE. Shit I'm dripping

VOICE. But better for it to have been and gone than to never have even been.

Which struck Kate deeply and shortly after her dad died, lying in bed with Rob and feeling hollowed but held, the sudden realisation of her mother's sudden poverty.

KATE. This is what she's lost after longer than I've lived.

VOICE. Brigid, though Kate couldn't have known this then, was trying to sleep alone above a table covered in paperwork and thinking –

BRIGID. I can still go to choir and sing but I'm scared it'll feel empty and who would I come home to, and if I went to the pictures now then who would I go with?

Will I meet new people or have I forgotten how to, and I don't want to not dance but I don't want to dance without you.

Is this the end of tenderness, will I be kissed again? Will I be held again?

Will our home ever feel like one, whether sad or happy, or will I always be waiting for something that's never going to happen?

You've left nothing of normal in this house but its ghost. What am I supposed to do with your shoe size or your shirt collar, the way you like your steak done or your hand held or not to be talked to at the pictures, what do I do with that?

What do I do with that tune you always hummed and I think is called 'The Best is Yet to Come', it might be but at the same time it definitely isn't.

You've made trivia of my memory of you and there's no quiz I can win with it.

VOICE. Things haven't been as awful as she feared they might be, but she hasn't been dancing, because dancing was their thing.

It was how they first met, through the weekly ritual of partnering for sets in some dancehall somewhere, and her crowd of pals rowed over which one every week.

DANCER 1. Peter's?

DANCER 2. The Olympic?

DANCER 3. The Crystal?

DANCER 4. The Four Provinces?

DANCER 1. The boys aren't respectful

DANCER 2. Fair point let's not go there

DANCER 3. The boys aren't respectful

DANCER 4. Fair point let's go there

VOICE. Regardless of location, she loved the quaintness of the faintly courtly language, as shirt-and-jacketed boys advanced like it was a Gallipolian landing towards the waiting ranks of lasses in their best dresses and fanciest shoes.

DANCER 1. Would you do a line?

DANCER 2. I would and all!

DANCER 3. You dancing?

DANCER 4. You asking?

VOICE. And the barefaced boys who dared to say things like

DANCER 1. That's a dancer's 'flank' you've got on you there

DANCER 2. I don't suppose you'd 'like some air'?

DANCER 3. Or to 'take a walk'?

DANCER 4. Your friend then, do you think she'd like to?

VOICE. Even if she didn't dance she still loved to watch, the many bodies moving like massed compassed pencils, describing arcs marklessly but surely on the floor, as the guitars wailed purely and the sax barked beautifully in red-hot numbers where the drummer got to cymbal snare and tom as manylimbedly as a foreign god or octopus.

DANCER 1. Forward forward left left

DANCER 2. Back back right right

DANCER 3. Slow slow

DANCER 4. Quick quick

Some god's thumb licked and slicked across the chalk of them as they blurred in her whirling eyes.

The sweet taste of spot-prize chocolate from the judges and twenty Player for her red-faced and gracelessly wheezing partner.

That's something she thinks of often, when she thinks of Frank.

How they danced for the first time when she was eighteen, he five years older, and how she flusteredly tried to lead and put his hand on her shoulder and her hand on his waist, but he just laughed it off, as graceful as she hadn't been.

How he started to look for her, and she for him in symmetry, till they slipped from hoping to see the other to going where they knew they'd be.

BRIGID. Hello.

FRANK. Hello.

BRIGID. Hello though.

FRANK. Hello then.

VOICE. How later her mother would watch the children, and they'd escape for a few hours of divvilment. Even in the years when she was angry with him they still danced weekly and cheek-to-cheekly and he'd hum the song like it had been written for them.

She thinks of that often.

But right now she hears the key and door turn and open, and is afraid for a moment when a man calls –

ROB. Brigid?

VOICE. So she knows she knows him, but when he comes into the room it's the same thing all over, she knows she knows his face but can't put a name to it, and so she stabs at it like its a maths problem –

BRIGID. He's a young man and he's talking to me which means he's probably –

'Michael!'

ROB. Rob actually, Kate's fella?

BRIGID. Sorry.

ROB. You're grand like, it happens to the best of us.

VOICE. And now she remembers, as Rob helps her get her coat on, she is two times a grandmother.

They bullet in a gunbarrel down the M1, they hello with Kate her daughter and wait for her son to wake.

And when he does Kate asks –

KATE. Do you want to hold him?

VOICE. And Brigid says

BRIGID. Of course I do.

VOICE. This has happened before with Kate the baby, Brigid the mother, and her mother the mother's mother.

And now she asks, as she was once asked and asked about herself –

BRIGID. What's his name?

VOICE. They tell her.

And whatsoever movement of the mouth they gift if not
christen him with is a history, a story, a link to something so
much more than he is, for now.

It might be Frank or Alan, for one of the grandfathers he'll
never know.

It might be biblical, for all that his parents aren't believers,
a Joshua, a Jacob, a Paul or Luke or Jesus or maybe even
an Adam.

But that's one tiny legacy in a room that's full of it.

These people are and were young thrice, grown twice, old
once, and they hold more than a century of sights and sounds
and gasps and grasps and tastings, a fortune has passed
through their hands in the form of their nights and days spent
whether spendthriftly or frugally, isolatedly or conjugally,
laughing gasishly elatedly or Picassoishly blue and gloomily.

This, now, these, all of them, is the pinch in the hourglass,
nadir and zenith of the gyre and gyre of present and past like
pyramids or roses, which grow or unfold as just-gone and
just-to-come moments exponent into numberless vastness, as
the near nighs, the nigh nexts, the next nows and passes.

And now it's past, but that's still true.

She asked his name, and they told her, and then she said

BRIGID. Lovely.

ZERO AGAIN

VOICE. It is later again than the late hour that happened, and
Rob is dropping Brigid home again. They sit without
speaking in the engine's rumble, the stillness broken only by
the metronome glint as they glimpse each approaching cat's
eye, and the car fills and empties with the light of each
passed-by lamp on the roadside.

En route they're rudely jolted when a taxi last-minutely bolts
from his lane into their one, and caught off-guard if not
unawares Rob brakes abruptly.

And Brigid says –

BRIGID. Sacred Heart

VOICE. Out of ancient habit, and he says –

ROB. Fuck you pal!

VOICE. And then he says –

ROB. Sorry Brigid

VOICE. And –

BRIGID. You're fine!

VOICE. She reassures him.

And though they don't know this, in the taxi our pal with the
family has just growled –

TAXIDAD. Fuck you too pal!

VOICE. He's just left home and hoves as do droves of his
fellows towards the the first fare of the night.

The driver – whose name, if you like, could be the same as
the baby's – hastens into tonight's game of stuck-in-the-mud
or chasing, he's yet to find out which.

He hums off-keyly, wandering freely from street to lamp and headlit street and from pitch to approximate pitch.

The tune, if you like, can be 'The Best is Yet to Come', it might be and it might be.

His headlights move amongst headlights like fish in an aquarium, at various junctions various marks of punctuation, comma colon or semi- or full-stopping the flow of traffic, cars letters in the letter the city writes and self-addresses, both speaking and spoken.

His night's beginning, so let's us stop before we start again, let's let the curtain and moon fall and rise on all of this open and closing, the wing and locket-like clasp and unfurling of lives lived like rockets rocket lonelily one-way and one-way only into the unknown of everything that will be but isn't yet.

Let's us stop, even if time won't, because time, like rain or a passenger or yesterday, never comes back but comes again.

It is night and here is the city, sleeping.

BOYS AND GIRLS

Boys and Girls premiered at The Pearse Centre, as part of Dublin Fringe Festival 2013.

A	Ronan Carey
B	Seán Doyle
C	Maeve O'Mahony
D	Claire O'Reilly

Director	Dylan Coburn Gray
Lighting Designer	Ilo Tarrant
Operator	John Gunning
Publicity/Marketing	Carla Rogers

Characters

A
B
C
D

Note on Text

The play has four (and a bit) chapters. It's roughly circular.

A B C D / D A B C / C D A B / B C D A / A

The audience is always there. If you're not speaking, you're listening.

A. Man's best friend: Google Chrome Incognito.
Nothing sweeter than a guaranteed pornless history, my dick
the victor who writes it and it writes mysteries. You'll never
know what went down – oh ho – and *fuck* now I'm thinking
about Agatha Christie. Instant boner-kill.

Spankwire, thank you, welcome distraction. Get some gentle
action going, up and down and up and down to the bottom of
the page where it says hey, April O'Neill? Good choice,
we're feeling that, but yer outta luck bub. Two vids, both old,
try Pornhub.

A pop-up offers a top-up on my penis, quick! Hop up on the
table and shazoom! Ladies can't resist your mister's va-va-
voom. They'll jump for that Topman-chinos-lump when they
spy with an admiring little eye a gee-busting hump-snake like
a lesser man's thigh. Swoon. Mr Tackle is knee-deep in poon.

Maybe not, thanks. Happy with what I got, thanks. No
illusions, me, about being – (*Exaggeratedly masculine
voice*.) a virile Rambo what shot tanks in some war. Nah, I'm
a weedy cunt from Dublin 4, gifted only with a mortally
offensive tongue and not the type to finish fights the barbed
fucker's begun.

Finish up with my modest manbits. Filthiest of habits, or
healthy self-love-affair? Best not ask my socks. Dress with
considerable care because my lack of muscle
notwithstanding my branding does what hustle does for
hunks. I present an uncompromising cynicism to the world,
ciggy in hand, smoke rising, two fingers unfurled. Girls are
intrigued, flattered by small attentions: the simple lack of the
typical verbal batterings means they might be in my league.
In there like swimwear. Yes, it's a play on insecurity; yes,
treat 'em mean keep 'em keen; but my ability to get a hand
up a dress at Alchemy is unmatched by the virtuous. True
love's path ever did run tortuous, hatcheted through briars or

hazarded with liars or both. Quoth this maven: the fires of
passion will swallow you whole. Safer to safeguard the ol'
ticker and just get yer – if you follow – hole.

Unless it's – well. Fucking hell, the merest mention of my
dearest Laura cranks the fucking tension for me because
she's a sight for sore eyes at the worst of times and at her
best she's a burst of pure – Jesus, yeah. If love is a sure and
willful self-abnegation, Laura's a sexy form of zen
meditation: inducing intimations of the transcendent in men
when she smiles. Her lines are fine enough for double-takes,
often double-taken for a model and who's to say you're
mistaken? She could would should be. So it's easy to think
she's beautiful because she's blonde, thin, shape of a violin
to fucking boot. Blah blah blah, *dutifully capitulating to
what society deems attractive*, that shit's just haters hating,
argument from those lacking the lack that Laura's rack alone
is lacking. Need a minute for that one? I'll spend it in
contemplation, because that lackless rack is crack-a-lacking.

Am I coming across laddish, big baddish wolf hoping to eat
her? In touch with my inner neanderthal, my soul wears a
wifebeater? (*Exaggeratedly masculine voice.*) *Equal rights
equal fights, chance of jobs is chance of no jobs, end of the
day what they're for is making sandwiches and blowjobs?*
Yeah. Unashamed. Got my Misogyny Club member's card
laminated and framed. Find my humour distasteful, crass,
dated? I find it wasteful when your mouth moves and my
penis remains unfellated. I crack me up.

Unless you're Laura, of course, for whom I'd turn
chivalrous. Come out of the castle to nearest and dearest and
mount up a white horse headed due timorous, servile,
mannered. I'd fly the banner for niceness and resultant
identity crisis be damned.
(*The gag is he's gay, only instead of being gay he's
a shithead.*)
But son, we thought your deal was… misanthropy.
There's no easy answer here; I thought so too.
Have you tried just… not being nice?
All my life, but something was missing.

Namely: Laura's hugging and kissing. And I'd settle for less.
I'd respect the shit out of her, and we'd both stay dressed. I'd
admire her intellect all night long, talk Dylan songs, put string
quartets on. Drink a nice wine till she begged for mercy,
maybe watch a romcom sans excessive cursing. The finer
things for this fine china lady, and my real Slim Shady
wouldn't dream of standing up. Nothing so abruptly sexual for
Laura, for I adore her without expectation or exception,
nothing so uncouth. For her if no one else I'm full of ruth, not
ruthless, and who's to know it's all a truthless evil façade? So
sociopathic deception feels a bit bad, I admit, but not as
tragically shit as I feel now. Haven't seen her in weeks and
you could literally plough with the hard-on I'm harbouring.

I think I'm incapable of love. But it's mistakeable for a certain
kind of hopeless attraction? A perseverance in the face of a
dearth of action, well known to the dicks with Dax on their
hair who like Laura but not like I do. I view their antics with
amusement, because it's not clear who's meant to be chasing
who. Coiffed and toned they may be, but able they're not for
the finely honed madness for the sake of laughs of my slick
surreal baby. On a dance floor she stands on their feet and
yells blue murder. BLEGH. It's fuckin' scary, and their
advances generally don't advance much further.

Though I've got it too. Fucking state of me. Unrepelled by
my beautiful mate and no more in her bonkers glory, I mean
I know all too well what's our story, but tonight I'm out,
tonight she's out –

B. Though out means a house, and predrinks means at least
three drinks stolen from Shane's parents' store. I'm pretty
sure there's a reason no one's drunk ketchup and absinthe
together before? But sher fuck it, with any luck it'll run out
soon and we can move on. Head out get the groove on and
get the rocks off, knock the ladies' socks off. And more!
If you know what I mean? Fellas for Barry, he can't marry
them but he fucks like a dream. Allegedly. Bear in mind my
lack of authority. This is conjecture, sadly, a projection from
the origin of the graph of promiscuity, casual sex being not
exactly my scene.

I've had one partners precisely, from six to nineteen and
though we treated each other nicely that doesn't mean it was
educational. Sex was less than sensational. Ali's comfort zone
ended before so much as talking matters masturbational, and
I wasn't any more open. Both of us shy, hoping the other
would start that convo: We didn't. Things moved on though,
regardless, awkwardly, hard to be smooth when you're not
sure should you talk or be silent, be rough or be kind when
your hand's here or there or where the fuck does it even go?
How the fuck am I supposed to know? Never occurred to me
at the time she might fake, and now that I'm single it's a curse
to me that I've taken no criterion for here on in by which to
make judgements. Or guesses. Am I doing anything with these
tender caresses or is she bored? Self-assured I am not, dating
leaves me feeling more frigid than hot, more mortifyingly
rigid than shot through with languid cool. Even getting the
shift requires a sangfroid I lack. Because back when others
were learning to navigate this ocean, to turn their expectant
face like a sextant to the north barman and motion to their
wingman? I was in man. There already. Girlfriend from my
mixed school, going steady. Who needs clubs or scoring or the
ride when relationships take work?

Now I'm stranded. Compassless. Without the first fucking
clue what one does to get humped, kissed or numbered.
Stumped by being single. And things only get worse,
because I'm modern, mild, PC. Uncomfortable with wild
sex, speech acts that betray internalised misogyny. (I can't
say cunt.) I am very much the middle-class progeny of Mr
and Mrs Untraumatic, Mr Staid Mrs Static, the one an
architect and the other a doctor of philosophy.

Raised to respect women and Kant, no anti-enlightenment
rape jokes for me, so bant be damned and so long easy
popularity. Queer? Not a weapon, not a barb, not an epithet
in my arsenal, it's a valid stance against heteropatriarchy.
Making a gas innuendo of 'epithet in my arsenal' is beyond
me. A black man walks into a bar: and why shouldn't he?
I never had a chance to not be that guy, the twat with the
political agenda even less cool than twitchy culchie Enda in

the fucking Dáil. Can't cope at ALL with the words
motherfucker, ho, harlot, or bitch, turn a mortified scarlet at
the idea of coming on your tits. Let alone your face! I'd be
disowned, disgraced, *no son of mine enacts hate with his
ejaculation!* Face on your mates when they're enjoying a
dead-baby joke or eight and you're the one going *take it
easy, yeah, bit insensitive?*

So no offence, Ma, love you loads Da, but you moulded me
too wholesome – too winsome and then some – to ever
fuckin' get some.

C. Let someone else do it, the frape is an artform. Bless ye,
Leah, you've got to be heartless. Gender change to start
with: Jen is now a dangler, stubbled and enlangered, a red-
blooded fan of girls angling for attention with Polaroids
parading both bad self-image and pretention.
Fuck's sake, my make-up is awful, I look shit.
'Jen' says *no, not at all*, 'Jen' says 'Jen' would wank to this.
Three people like. Lol.
REAL Jen says we're cunts, all of us, back from the jacks,
and Leah unceremoniously slaps her round the head.
FUCKING OW.
I hate the word cunt. Leave it out.

But all the names are naff or disgusting, laughable or pushing
the bounds of decency. Leah says recently her ma's been using
'ladygarden' as a joke, but the humour hardly outweighs the
hopeless cringe. Minge is gross. The room's mostly in favour
of 'gee', with Jen owning to some uncertainty. Axe-wound,
gash, beef curtains: unanimously vetoed.
Vagina's very gyno, kind of too cold and matter-of-fact.
Always comes across a little clinical, like you've just been
speculumed or diagnosed with the clap.
You're certain about beef curtains? I think it's funny. (I'm
alone in that.)
But then, I *like* cunt. Try to contain yourselves. I like that it's
unsellable in a world where sex sells. Dirty, yeah, but a million
miles from sexy or flirty, it's not pussy. This is a word with
aggression to burn and its hustle on. It remains the eleven on

the Spinal Tap amp, the building in your college with no
wheelchair ramp. (It's inaccessible.) The Saxon grunt of it
caresses like a gothkick in New Rocks, much more powerful
than dicks langers lads or cocks. They're small silly words,
ye'd almost say them to yer granny: childish, belittling, less
cunt more fanny. Bless.

Boys may use it, can't own it, can't make it less. It loses no
impact in the white cis male mouth, be he butcher, baker,
literary-theory-maker, commerical mover and shaker or pissed
stag-night lout. Which is why porn prefers pussy. Because
cunt is uncompromising. When a john himself and he find
their old chap rising and they're looking to get busy, cunt
spoils the mood. Sexual, but not sexy, it intrudes on this most
sacred of sacreds, this loving act of self-hatred – if you believe
the Church – with the unwelcome reality. He's no god of sex,
he's odd-looking, face kind of bandy. He's unemployed to
boot, his next job is this joyless handy-fucking self-
administered, and from behind this blistered-palm onanism
looks like bestiality. Is that too harsh?

Cunt means his hate, and hate's the hard drug that's gatewayed
by his fear, and fear's a bummer of an E-number that boys
take in with mother's milk and milkshakes and beer. All their
lives! Cunt is insecurity, a sign he's not sure that he belongs in
the dick-club. It's his fear of inadequacy, of white male
privilege unveiled as travesty, of everyone knowing he can't
get hard as he wanks, that he's not some hyper-macho tank
with a semi-perma-semi-stiff-or-stiff. You get me? Never
flaccid. Gender's a massive bitch – oh the irony – and she spits
corrosive acid at your soul. Want to be her friend with
benefits? Gotta try to adhere to the mould, got to fear, got to
hate who and what you're told to because if they're less then
we're more, if we're sexual subjects they're whores, if we're
normal, they're queer, we're it they're un-, *cockito ergo cunt*
ergo hateful denigration of all undicked, the woman the gay
man the sissy the gay chick whether leather-clad or no,
screaming queen or pass for heteronormal, anyone threatening
the good old status quo. This is our game, you spoil it, off to
jail faggots and do not pass go.

So take it! (Cunt.) For fuck's sake, own it. Best fucking way
to dethrone it! Turn their hate round, lube its arse up and
bone it! Is that unfeminist? I'm preaching love, I swear.
Learn to say cunt. Learn not to care. What more have they
got? Learn to love not the message but its container, rise
above the hate and redress wrongs with raunch-making,
taking yourself spread-eagled on your bed shouting cunt.
Undress and showerhead yourself silly, grunt and grind to
nirvana. Cunt. Cunt. Cunt. Cunt. Cunt.

Don't worry about their contempt, for redemption comes
when you do. The voodoo of getting off on degradation kills
its sting. Call me a bitch, call me a cunt, call me any fucking
thing, see what it does to me. Your terror when your Enola
Gay crashes and the gashes take the day is cunting poetry.

No one answers, but then no one expected –

D. A text from an ex who I'm kind of still friends with.
   Out tonight? Xo
   A very good question, and the answer's a laugh. The
   boyfriend's gaff, so technically out, fun with showers of
   awkward expected.

Long-term endeavour, this. Friends first, that bubble burst
by a kiss. My doing, and I nearly missed his lips and got his
nose. He drew back mostly because he was startled,
I suppose, or hope, but asked no questions. Things are best
when they require no explanation and run no risk of hurt
feelings. (*Exaggerated Dublin accent.*) Meetin'. Does what
it says on the tin. I think I initially fancied him more than he
did me, really, but why say so when there ain't no way to do
so tactfully?

And he was the one who L-bombed me, as a matter of fact,
an 'I love you' served with no dose of cautious irony.
Three months two days, drunk on Jim's bed:
*Let me count the ways, fuck that like, that's bollocks, simplest
is best. Though it's interesting that 'I love you' has come to
mean less, right? Though I think that's changing, right?
Maybe we're on the cusp of the new sincerity, an age where*

it's verity that counts and not form. Fuck 'fucking the norm',
right, hipsters can go stand in a fucking thunderstorm.
(Exaggerated hipster voice.) 'Comfort's been done.'
Unashamed by cliché, what I mean is I love you.
The feeling wasn't reciprocated. Not proud, not something to
be said aloud, that he was falling on ears untitillated by his
tender whispers. Bit of a nightmare: he's sweet he's kind he's
smart, I know I should but I don't care.

But then, 'I love you'. Push comes to shove you don't even
know what you mean.
You're attractive, and your personality's not shit?
At eighteen the reality is that that applies to anyone with tits.
(It's amazing what people fail to see when they're blinded by
the blazing corona on a pair of ecliptic apocalyptic double Ds.)

Well.
I'll own up, Cs.
Bordering on Bs.
Interesting fact: lack of pride in an A is common only to bras
and Junior Cert CSPE.

Love? Need. I plead guilty to some cynicism in this, that love
is less kiss or frisson of feeling and more someone who'll aloe
vera your sunburn when it's peeling. Meaning family are often
good for that shit, because they've seen you at your batshit
worst and know just to batten down the hatches, but it's
frowned on when your needs come to include someone to go to
town on – if you know what I mean – to continue to lean on
your next of kin for such. *Game of Thrones*, much? And for me
Jamie became that. I'm ashamed that it took so long, brooked
so much wavering. Save that I'd said it already and lied,
he'd've died a thousand times waiting for that 'I love you'.

'I love you' meaning mutual reliance plus mutual lust.
Do what you want to me!
but also:
DO WHAT YOU MUST.
It doesn't sound as beautiful or graceful put that way, but
fuck beauty and grace because when we met my nana was
starting to forget faces and places and think I was her sister.

These things ought to be clean and easy: no queasy
apprehension moment by moment, hoping against hope for
some mercy, some surcease of cruelties like my mother's
casual-but-who-do-you-think-you're-fooling *She never
recognises me any more*.
My Leaving to be done, and my mother unfit to give a shit
beyond her mother's unravelling.

So yeah, things were tense, and it was immensely helpful to
have something – someone – to escape to. Jamie was all but
caped and extra-jocked, my softly spoken superhero shocked
I'd think anything of the hours I spent lying spent on his
shoulder. Prone to proneness, and he nice enough to pretend
it not onerous.

And yeah, sex. A first for me, a first for he, and first associated
acts with worse publicity. (Remembering your first handjob
fondly's an eccentricity, I'm told. But sex should be life-
changing? I'm not entirely sold.) Sex. Exclusivity is
important. For sure, it's not love *per* se, but the above being
proved means we must first prove for one. Not THE one, I'm
no Christian, but this was a departure, finding a reason to trust
as I hadn't before. Speaking candidly, I don't trust well. If
A then B, if T then he's a candidate for L. Loss of V-plates
isn't insensate amorous bliss, exactly, but its occurrence
betokens that this is a new thing, a true thing, and that clichéd
words oft spoken might finally be felt.

A. It's pelting rain but I'm in Twisty P, I'm twisted, I'm dancing
   to house –

B. Yesses all round to a further three bottles ousted from
   Shane's parents' stash –

C. Heading to the dollar signs for esses of Hussle in Buttoner –

D. At Jamie's, and Jamie gets put-upon with others in the
   kitchen so I should probably just sit and pick a CD. Not as
   easy as it sounds: Jamie frowns on no genre, hates to genre-
   lise about rap rock or pop, but he's a classical boy in that
   he's rapt for what he likes and apt to bitch all night if not.
   Laura Marling passes muster so I bust out her latest.

Two years today, his 'rents out of town and the way.
Capital-R ROMANTIC, but there's this awkward hashtag
bedroom-antics vibe we can't quite dispel. Because an
empty house is rare for us, so there's this expectation we'll
raise hell, give it welly, break the bedsprings, it wasn't
good unless you made things shake with your screams.
But I'm quite quiet, so not in your wildest wet dreams.
And don't get me wrong, our non-ability to play it cool's
not frigidity at work. Nothing Herculean, but there are
things which we are both quite good at, as one should at
this stage understand. But neither of us talks dirty and
Jamie can be awkward to beat the band. (He says, no joke,
almost ready!)

And that's true now too! As Laura moans her bed is empty
because this like all her albums is gloomy. Jamie has come
into the living room decrying his inability to cook. Really
I couldn't give a fuck, though we are eating fish fingers
'ironically'. Sashays to the kitchen and back with wine. Red,
from Lidl, cheap but fine for broke students. A toast to our
anniversary, ironic again, but a genuine toast to me, his best
friend, who listens to him shite on about Schumann. Right-
on, and it's a nice easy moment for a kiss. But now the fish
fingers are burning, and Jamie's learning the hard way that
even low-key irony needs a token level of care.

A. Phil had pills, and if they're there why not. Two –

B. Two –

C. Two –

D. Two –

A. Shots of Jäger chased it, and now my face is starting to work
and grin. Din of the bar is cut by teeth grinding and I'm
finding it so much easier to get into the tekkentechno now.
Not my scene but I respect the DJ, a fellow human being, no
matter what we say to the contrary there's nary a difference
between us really. Know what I mean? Know what I mean?
I am fierce in this conviction and a goth with a brow-piercing
and tequila-slurred diction knows what I mean. Right-on my
brother, we're all sons of mothers here. Mother dearest, I'm

glad you can't see me, lips working obscenely to the beat
like I'm eating out a rhino.

B. I'm trying to relax but this is fucking hell. MacTurcaill's
sells pints for three fifty to the thrifty student clientele.
Gotyercard?
Yes, but it's hardly necessary when the session's already
going, going, gone to the bathroom with Shane.
Three –

C. Three –

D. Three –

A. Three –

B. Pints. Pain in the bladder and orgasmic relief when emptied.
Shane's giving me grief for being a numpty, always
operating on the assumption that no one fancies me. Niamh
does, apparently.
*I've told you before and she's eyeing, she's fucking eyeing, so
don't be a dryshite.*

This is potentially my night made. Niamh is quiet and quite
intelligent, with the kind of elegant good looks that get passed
up for tits. She has them, but they're – it's – an incidental fact
next to her cheekbones, wit, warmth, smile. Yes, I'm a
sentimental dope, and while I know this I still can't stop.

Marky is doing his pill-head impression –
(*Exaggerated Dublin pillhead voice circa 2013.*) *AW
FUCKING WAIT FOR IT HERE COMES THE DROP.*
And Niamh is laughing while Aoife's scooting to let me sit
down. I'd be set if she'd just get up, go for a drink, think her
make-up needs a touch-up or something so that I could brush
up my arm against Niamh's, catch her eye, leave the group
chat for solo, be Han not some bozo who's secretly her brother.

Another drink, why not, and success yes we're in there,
adjacency achieved. Nerves.
Me being me I won't chase if she runs but sher roll up my
sleeves and break out my best line:
'Hi.'

No one's more surprised than me when it's easy.

C. Italians out in force tonight, sleaze running down the walls.
I'm not dancing, hip hop's a ball but not worth clumsy Latin
grinding. An erection from behind should be only by
invitation.

Breath on my face when Dave leans down from his vantage.
Six-foot-four, extensive bant at his expense is regularly had.
We measure things in Daves:
Save your breath, still got a kiloDave to walk.
What's pink and three millionths of a Dave long?
Dave's cock.
Do you want a drink?
In close by my ear. It's a bit weird, this, me and Dave have
history but not in any big way. Perhaps he thinks we'll segue
from drinks to chats to me flat on my back. Fat chance
tonight, hun, you can have a dance though, alright hun? In
exchange for this pint, like. Four –

D. Four –

A. Four –

B. Four –

C. I amn't the kind to hoard 'virtue', to call whore those who
flirt without intent to deliver. Live and let live or be bitched
about yerself. And anyway, shelf-life is overrated. Much
better to be wined, dined, dated, or, y'know, just fucked. It's
all good.

Speaking of, just my luck, here are Conor, Jen, Claire, and
Leah. Nice to see ya all but especially you, Conor, scholar of
Trinity College and phone-saboteur extraordinaire. His
favourite trick is to debonairly look-over-therely disarm you,
and then drop the bombshell that *hush hush hush don't be
alarmed or ashamed, but I've been in your contacts and
swapped yer da's and fella's names.*

With no irony, he's an unrepentant cunt. Unapologetic for
my texts sent to my Rory meant for Da, or for abhorrent
sexts meant for the buachaill that went Da-ward.

Well. Rory's history. And Conor's Amy is unmissed in our
lives for some months now. And that's not unrelevant

because it crosses my mind. Conor may be evil but it's my
kind and I like him despite myself. Chain-smoker with an
elfin nose, pointy like his conversation. Blows pretention
from the water, deflates sensationalism and self-heroicising
alike. Deeply copped-on but makes free with his gays,
bitches, retardeds. Hard to see he cares deeply but doesn't
care for right-on types and circle-jerk fawning. In short, the
kind of guy I'd do the nasty with till morning.

And might yet, fingers crossed.

D. It's alright, I tell him, informal was the idea. But even for our
relaxed notion of normal this is pushing it. I agree that big
romance is taxing and fussy, unrealistic, but it's a bit shit if
you can't even do mockery right.
The night's ruined, eh?
He grins, which is intended to hide the fact he's actually
worried what I'll think, if I'll tear him a new one while on
the brink of hopeless tears.
I can cope, hun.
His fear allayed, we opt for a film and Chinese. *Kiss Kiss
Bang Bang*, Robert Downey Jr. always pleases.

He's still worried, so I hang off his neck while he's setting
up, stop him getting up, mess fight kicks off. His best move
is squishing me, his weight deliciously atop me to stop me
moving. Or breathing. Grab his nuts and and now he's
leaving off, not daring to so much as cough or sneeze.
MERCY PLEASE MERCY.

Mild sadism makes me thirsty, so we finish the wine. Take
away in five.

A. Five –

B. Five –

C. Five –

D. Night's on form now, lying calm and slightly drunk against
his side.
Michelle Monaghan's a ride
I say. He prefers Val Kilmer, fat Batman though he may be.
Save me from boys who think gay flirting is funny.

Chow mein. When we're done so is Rob, got the girl did the job. It's just now twelve, how insane is our life.

A. Upstairs rife with indies, their quiffs stiff with indescribable potions, and their disaffected going through the motions looks like a Jedward-flavoured tsunami. This balmy sweatbox is not to my taste, and though my pulse is racing it's the pills and not the ultra-camp scream of electro synth. If androids do dream then they wet dream this filth and enjoy it.
Is that Phil?
I feel ADHdestroyed by the lovebuzz, can't focus see or talk straight or shove past this cunt outside the jacks. Ah let's face facts, he's not so bad, the sadsack's pretending to text cos he's been left by his mates. The poor dear. I'd give him a hug only fuck, Laura's here, bad I'm still this up I should chill out but I can't because Ben's ranting in my ear. Sometimes being peerless seems attractive. Act natural, natural, natural that way she'll not cop anything's up.
So you guys are mashed as fuck.
Rumbled, but we're heading to the tumult of the basement where the bass melts faces and drinks get spilled. Is this my sixth?

B. Six –

C. Six –

D. Six –

A. Thirty-year-old goths and sixteen-year-olds trying Es are mingling to D and B, and the gap between she and me is narrowing. Vibrations in my bone marrow feel orgasmic and this thought has to be shared, who cares if its E-spiel because she's feeling it too, I mean she's had something for sure or else what's she blurry for?

Rub my eyes furiously and move us to the dance floor where Ben's entranced by an interplay of snare and kick and he's tripping into me and the gap between me and she is widening as she laughs. Ben's an asshole and it requires much self-control not to hand his to him. Though I do love him.

FUCKING CHOON
he bleats, and the beat insists that I concur, this is
murderously mortally deadly, the music goes straight
through my head and turns to colour, and suddenly full of
fucks to give I shiver with the intensity of this moment
because I know when she leans in she's going to say
Smoke?
And I say yes, suddenly full of an inexpressible irrepressible
hope that bubbles over, because a ciggy and a chat is the
perfect means of showing her I'm the coolest mofo going.

B. Conversation's flowing ridiculously well. Talking about anger,
and how neither of us has a gift for it. Take many's the
crashdummyish hit for it when hell breaks loose and stuff gets
real. She feels it's mostly used as an excuse to go apeshit, to
make shit dramatic, to pull out all the stops and loose the mad
wife in the attic. Intense feeling's enjoyable, and to have it's to
want to use it, abuse it, as anyone with a penis or a gun knows.
Her comparison, and her sense of fun shows through the fact
that she's spot-on. I'm nodding because I haven't gotten on
like this with anyone in forever, regardless of whether I'm
scoring. And what's more the drink is flowing but I don't think
I'm talking shite? Seventh –

C. Seven –

D. Seven –

A. Seven –

B. And normally I'd be level on my back but instead I'm
levelling with her that as a kisser I'm neither famed nor
ashamed because let's face it who is? I've never disgraced
myself, at least, and she's laughing and saying she has. First
spazzy kiss at fourteen, and machine-like's an understatement.
Her tongue went numb from his braces and the repeat bionic
movement, and is it completely off-base to say this chat and
platonic are not aligned? Nothing's delivered, sealed, or
signed, but I've this shivering apprehension. So I'm loath to
let her go when she says she needs the bathroom, and Barry
swoops in and asks me am I hopeful. And for fear of being

boastful I say not really. Which means really, imagination roaming freely into a future bright with good things.

C. Flirting, and should things continue I won't be sorry. Conor's reputedly a torrid machine, and this is disputed only by Jen who's his ex. But then what does one expect from someone who compulsively fucks boys over herself.

Safe with a posse we've shouldered towards the DJ, drinks clutched and clutches dumped for ease of dancing so that we sway unencumbered. Conor's hand strokes my lower back, and this is light touch number three. This story's growing clearer, and his pelvis edges nearer as beats drop and drops of sweat threaten to pollute pints. Jen shoots filthies at me and Conor shouts
What's she at, she's the one who dumped me.

For the sake of clarity let's affirm that this is no possessive flirtation, no vengeance vendetta or aggravated GBhatecrime. I always would have made time for Conor had she not claimed him. And if he's single and I'm the same then take our word it isn't personal. Stand assured of that, and back off with the aggro, it's several agos that yiz ended. You is friended, bitch, and this fight staying unfought will be soonest mended. It's NOT ABOUT YOU.

The bar for number eight –

D. Eight –

A. Eight –

B. Eight –

C. And while we wait he respectfully enquires what my plans are. If the band are moving on do I think I'll follow split or stay? Raise our drinks and hollow clink and shit, I say, I just don't know now. He screams
Should I stay or should I go now?
and so now I've a reason to 'mishear' him and endear him to my profile by leaning in sideways. *What?*
His fingers march in slow file up my back and onto my face and he tugs on my ear. Funny, but weirdly arousing as well.

His apartment's just off Harcourt, and now he's tellingly
offered housing should I have nowhere else to crash.
Reading between the lines he'll lash it into me if I so wish.
Consider. I know this fella and he's not crazy, more dishy
lady- than fishy serial-killer. I kinda want this.
Let's be up front
I say,
is this a spare-bed job or jobs-of-the-head kind offer?
He coughs and says
Which would you prefer?

Getting busy is thus on the cards.

But having come this far and established we're playing, why
delaying and bluffs? Got the cards, that's enough, get your
coat don't fluff and waver. Why wait for him to get drunker
and his chap to get shrunker and his fingernails no blunter?
Grab this, now.

D. And it's here on the couch –

A. And outside is freezing, damp from it pissing down –

B. Smoking in the cold with Niamh, ostensibly missing out
but not –

C. And I've sensibly decided I won't be going home. Warn
Claire to phone me in the morning, check I'm not murdered.
His hallway now, going further to the living room as are we,
kissing deeply entwinedly with free-roaming hands, and the
bra is candidly boldly unhooked.
Cheeky fuck
I say. And he waves that away with an
'Advance problem-solving.'

D. And now the kiss is evolving I find I'm undissolved. Not
a quivering shivering puddle of lust, the effort of frenzied
thrusting feels beyond me. His hand on me is doing nothing,
just feels comfy.

A. My plumed smoke plays footsy with hers and disperses.
A bouncer next door curses at crowds of Propagandists,
bare-legged cleavaged sixteen-year-old fans of the Coronas

and The Script. Shivering in the night, nips straining tiny
dresses. Lads mad on bravado and professions of guy love.
I ventriloquise a
Why, bud, why?
over this young guy in the gutter, and I'm utterly chuffed that
Laura deigns to find this funny.

B. And it's unreal how painfully sexy her cigarette is, this
transient pet that she dotes on for two minutes. Whatever
way you spin it this feels private, this feels like I've gotten
in there. She stubs out and smooths hair and closes eyes, and
I suppose I'm supposed to take this chance to have a look.
Fuck, I'm drunk.
And I've sunk in my lean so we're level, our faces close the
rabble chatter of other smokers feeling distant. AND. NOW.
WE'RE. KISSING. Though I'm pissed beyond reason it's
still ecstatic.

C. The brat has a talent for this kind of teasing, a taloned rake
of my breast with a pleasing pressure, better for the presence
of his fingernails. (Which are short.) But this still entails a
brief catch on my nipple, a roughness a stippling of his glide
across my flesh and it's best when he leans in and means it a
bit mean. Kiss remains firm clean direct bites my lip and his
erection's rising nicely.

This is the kind of thing I'd – almost – come from.

D. No pleasant thrum of tension, this G-string is untightened and
remains bent on a good night's sleep. I have no problems with
libido, I'd quite like sex. But unexpectedly he's not on form. If
I let on though he'll fall heedless into worry, hurry to the big
moves, try to whip up the storm. But really we'd be better off
holding off till morning. The pressure to be loved-up and
bowled over's a pain. And if you don't respond it's more effort
again. Makes me feel like a bitch which I amn't.
Was it something I did? Something I said?
I take matters into my own hands and say I want to give
him head.

Which is a lie. Happy anniversary!

A. And I'm versed in what I should do to seduce, but I'm fruitlessly wavering because the buzz is wearing off and my confidence with it. Laura nods down the road to where Propaganda's just closed and so exploded. Teenage exhibitionists piss, kiss, get fingered. An integral part of the Dublin nightlife experience. Fuck you Academy, and your maddening acceptance of emos and belvoids, of swell roides and teen hos. You're ruining my night because Laura's sighted one that we know.

B. And we're going going gone again, hand on her skin her back curves upon the wall of this streetlet where we've hid. Alley sounds so riddled and classless, but ask us and we'd tell you it's for lack of choice. We both live at home, we've no coy secret signs amongst housemates to say sex is happening. That'd be unhappy for all concerned, bridges burned as regards our privacy. And so we continue indiscriminately, in this public but as private as possible place. This isn't exhibitionism for the sake of goss and a high-five, this is great and precisely because so not to be shared with one's mates. The air's cold, her tongue fiery.

I'm wary of getting too into this, aware that this intimacy probably can't last. Arousal fades fast when opportunity is stymied. But this time with my hand warm between her thighs is golden, and her urgent stolen breaths are the best sound I've ever heard.

C. He's absurdly good, wood pressing against me, fingers send me to happy places. His face is pressed to mine, breath is mine and he gasps as I clasp him with legs around his waist. Begs a moment's grace to adjust and I tell him just take that shit off. I may have bit off more than's chewable, for his body's hot and smooth and pre-eminently do-able. He moves down mine with his lips to my stomach and my hips rise all on their own.

D. He moans soft, almost sighs, not vocal but totally absorbed in what I'm doing. A little to-ing a little fro-ing a little showing you're enjoying it and that's all it takes. Media make a big deal of it: it's degrading or disgusting but must we really take stances on love made in private? Jamie sometimes rebuffs me cos he can't believe I like to. And if I tried to explain that few do but few mind then he's the kind who'd not get it. I'd to train him to let it happen though he's happy to do me. Truly, he's too well behaved. So earnestly determined to save me the trouble he ends up selfish.

A. I can't help it, I say fuck. Just my luck that at this moment when closeness is closing the deal Neal shits all over us. My little brother's friend. Wojus drinker. Distinctly unsteady as he's ejected into the night, his fifteen-year-old liver wrecked on vodka or Jäger. He's shivering. The dote. I'll wager they only clocked he's a youngster when he chundered. Spatter down his front attests he's been sick. Messy and incapable of standing, much less getting home, he's staggering down the luas line on the brink of a sambuccoma. No choice really, I leave the smoking area to go to him.

Laura asks am I leaving –

B. And unbelievably she's asking do you have a condom. On me? I do, but who could have seen I'd be using it. And a whispering misgiving moves through me that this might not be the time or the place, that drunk cold loving is not likely to be graceful. But a chance like this should be chased down, as foxes are rare. Carefully tear the wrapping and this is where it gets awkward.

C. Talk to me he says so I vocalise rhapsodically, unchoked by thoughts of neighbours no shame in this moment. Prophylactic's on and the primary action is go and so –

D. And I know he's going to soon because he bucks with more urgency.

A. Familial emergency I smile, though I'm raging. Fuck responsibility.

B. Her clothes are disarrayed for… accessibility. But she's shorter than me so the angle is unfortunate. Can you skin your jeans down further?

C. It almost hurts, it's hard, but his ardour is tangible and because tangible tasty –

D. And his face twists and he warns me to get out of there, but I don't care enough to do so.

A. And he's too locked to even know me. it shows in his eyes, which are glass-like. Unfocused.
Neal?

B. And I hope this is it, but I'm guessing. And then she gasps –

C. And I say yes –

D. And he says yes –

A. And he says yes –

B. And yes I'm in –

C. And I say yes –

D. And I think yes –

A. And I think grand –

B. And now we're grand –

C. Fuck yes –

D. The taste –

A. It's fine –

B. We're fine –

C. And yes –

D. And no –

A. And yes –

B. And now –

C. And now –

D. And now –

A. And now –

B. And now –

A pause.

We're done.

Unspectacular. Should I act like I don't know it? Not exactly
expecting afterglowing praise. I was semi-hard at most. Too
many pints to boast of a godly display of prowess. Meaning
now it's time to tidy up, the only sound our loud unedifying
breath. Zip up, re-bra, best avoid eye contact. Act like
nothing happened, because what really can you say? Some
day again, never again, call me, don't? I won't – can't –
pretend that this was stunning, moving, that she came within
a mile of coming because I know. I know, alright?

It wasn't even nice. And you can't spoon after on a street.
Can't treat the other to a naked dance, prancing for
unselfconscious laughs. You just fuck. So what do you say?
Now it's over, sobered, the cold feels colder. And oh she has
a missed call from her buddy for the taxi, so we laxly
holding hands walk the few streets to Doyle's. Maybe this
contact's an unspoiled affirmation, but a look at her face and
I think it's more of an ending. A full stop.

C. And when he finally pulls out we breathe for a time, a
reasonless rhymeless nothing of satiation. Face to face and
I'm uncrushed, just cradled, unable to move for the
closeness. The moment ends when both of us awake to
different needs: he to drain the lake in his bladder and me to
have a smoke. Open a window and in blows a breeze that
bites love-sweat damp skin. He stamps in, now deflated,
elated and poses. Up on his toes, arms flexed, legs wide,
tackle flopping sexily side to side he roars:
Heyooo! High five.

Are you for real? Deadly serious. And here was me thinking
we were grown-ups. But he wants to own up now that he's
not, because it's much less fucking fun. And he's looking
unmoved, so I gracefully surrender and render unto the man-
child what needs to be rendered. High-five. He smiles, it's
contagious, I call him an outrageous wanker. He thanks me.

Finish my smoke, flop back down on the bed, head resting
on the pillow by his and he whispers
Oh, I just remembered a great thing.
I face him, say it better be, I'm waiting.

So until pretty recently, his friend hadn't done this. The
horizontal mambo. Got real drunk, libido flame-lit and
lambent, sees a likely girlo and tries some virginal unlikely
gambit. Success. No need to confess to inexperience, girl
sussed that it was new to him, was cool to him. Turns to him
when it's over and soberly announces
Condolences. You can't ride unicorns any more.

I laugh. Things are easy. Sleep comes teasing at my eyelids
so I just rest them as he speaks. Best to sleep some anyway,
heavy night's heavy day of explaining to do tomorrow.

But that's tomorrow.

D. As ever he was careful, stroked my hair, wasn't rough, it
wasn't tough just slightly tasteless. No compliments to the
chef. But yes, I was bored. Not to make this more than it is,
not to mountain this molehill, but I kinda wish I coulda told
him In The Morning And That's It. Not that I couldn't, but I
wouldn't because he'd be hurt, and wordless reproach is worse
than pressure. I wish he were better practised at rolling with
life's punches, knew that bad weather with fair isn't a bell
tolling for we. Sometimes you're angry and unreasonable and
everyone pees shits and farts and starts fights for no reason.
Happiness is seasonal and he's hopeless with winter. Can't
cope with a screaming match, and yeah sometimes I want one.
Nail him onto a cross with cross words and be forgiven
because to live with someone is to live with their bullshit their
flaws their 'sins'. Forgive me. Get the fuck used to it. But
Jamie's idea of happiness ends where mine begins.

I suppose we should break up, sooner or later, but to take up
this good thing and dash it down is beyond me.

A. Left her bereft of my wide-eyed company. This cunt needs
me more than she does, assuredly.
Where're your friends?
He's not sure, can't answer clearly. Shaking his head and
frowning. Where's there to go. Nowhere. Town is cold and
rainy, painfully unwelcoming to the underage and braindead.
And I've no money for a taxi. It wouldn't tax me to walk
him home, he's local, but his folks are gonna kill him –

awkward! – and I'm not sure he has a walk in him. Garda car imminent so I get him to come with me. The Londis with the Subway, with my last change get him water. It ought to help, can't hurt anyway. He's very much the worse for where can he lie down pronto, he's barely conscious.

Neal? Stay with me.

Honestly. Time to bear it while grinning. I hoist the skinny fuck by his waist and onto my shoulder and get marching. Smell of puke is distasteful but what can you do.

Who wouldn't? I couldn't not. Laura's great, but let's face it we're mates and no more, so why tempt fate or karma? The shame if harm came to him. Safe than sorry, thanks. Save on worry thanks. It might be a blurry line between good form and duty, it might be more normal for cute females to get the escort. But if this were my brother and not his buddy I confess I'd want him guarded. Seen home and saved from his own retarded carry-on. And regardless. Between pills and my arduous bout of self-loving, the hard-on's not turned on. No fire lit in this oven. Worth holding out to acquit oneself well. Some other time, fingers crossed. Or so I tell myself. Over and over as with his arm round my shoulder I Clontarf-wards trudge. Such is a night out.

And afterwards – he awake enough to life again to whine about bouncers – I take myself home unthanked, he thankless and thoughtless save of bottles left undrunk. Fifteen-year-olds on Stella, who'da thunk they'd be so cold.

Roll up home with the dawn, yawns cracking my face open. Look out over the coast road, where most of the city sleeps deep soft and peaceful. I've often felt this is the best time of day, when less time feels like more, when the two chimneys soar like brush strokes and you can see clean to Howth. Breathclouds like smoke. I make the most of it, chill in my garden in the brittle chill as dew forms and sun rises, and soon enough two forms pass, surprised to see me. Jogger and his dog catch my eye, nod a greeting.

Howya.

Not bad.

DRAWING CROSSES ON A DUSTY WINDOWPANE

For Claire Galvin
In memory of Dennis Galvin

Drawing Crosses on a Dusty Windowpane was first performed at the Mick Lally Theatre, as part of Galway Theatre Festival 2016, after a work-in-progress showing at Project Arts Centre, as part of the Dublin Fringe Festival 2015.

Performer	Claire Galvin
Director	Liam Halligan
Lighting Designer	John Gunning
Sound Designer/Composer	Sean James Garland
Producer/Publicity/Marketing	Carla Rogers

Note on Text

Spaces between blocks of text indicate pauses. These can be filled with music, or action, or left as a moment of consideration with/for the audience.

The audience is always there. If you're not speaking, you're listening.

This is a memory, a threnody, a memorial, an elegy,
they're all salves when you can't just McCartney and let it be.
When the hurt is unhalveable, no less or better whether kept
close or shared openly,
of a hopeless kind not tearable to pieces of peaceful mind. But
being seen to sing is at least less lonely: you can sing to
remember what's gone so it won't be.

This is London in January, and double as many undone
resolutions trouble this wired city as live in our entire republic.
The whitest month's bleakness is still equal to it,
correspondingly larger.

I am in a pub and my early twenties, nursing a lager on my
own, waiting for my best friend to join me. My phone rings.

For the last time with that ringtone: I changed it right after
hanging up, as the barchange and laughter laughed on and
clinked on.

My ma, once married to your older brother, had just told me
that you were dead.

I must have felt something, then and there, had some thought,
prayer or question pelt through my head to my mouth, but that's
lost to me. My friend arrived, I passed on the news because he
had known you, and we proceeded to throw back drink after
drink until we passed out and over the brink of forgetting.

I know these facts, but not what I felt, or thought.

Here's what I feel and think now:

That life is like a Junior Infant's butterfly painting. It unfolds
itself not into new newness, but old things made new. Ever so
neatly the patterns repeat themselves, now laterally inverted.
I am thirteen, in Cork, and my father dies in London.

A decade and then some, I am here in England, and an uncle almost more than parent dear to me dies there.

We're Cork, from a small town that Dublin would call *country*. But if our accent's black to the Jackeen's white then Towntalk's still Milkybar next to the Bogger's Crunchie.

How are you and *HOWARRU*.

Teeth and *TAITH*.

Peaches, BLAICHES.

King Crisps, KING TAYTO.

Fifteen hundred people now, and never before bigger. One main road, one school, but seven pubs purveying liquor. A not-so-lucky number, there used to be fourteen, and I don't know what mortal blow struck down but left seven.

An ex-cinema that sells couches nowadays, the holsterless gauchos of yesterwesterns themselves held up by upholstery.

A ball-less ballroom, where once buses bused in attendees in their hundreds, that remembers rocking for Dickie and rolling out red carpet for Joe Dolan, now locked up, dis-membered by disco.

Minus music or the pictures where do a lad and a lass go when they go out together?

Five out gay men, all under thirty or thereabouts, and one beangarda who flirts with me and no one's really sure about. Maybe they added something to the water in the eighties? Slipped in some man-but-not-woman-turning chemical, some infernal flipper of the internal switches that tell us if it's buachaills or bitches we desire. Or was it the arrival of Madonna, more like a fiery comet than a virgin, did the honours? Did she do it and do for the pubs into the bargain? Are the demise and rise of houses for drinking and men aroused by men perhaps linked?

Regardless. It's our town, and though you didn't grow up here, you visited not but nearly every summer. This town you were yearly the banterous talk of the planted stalk of a blooming life in London. First-generation Irish in England. Your mother and father, newly husband and wife, made the move together but never actually a life. Four years at the outside before your father, my grandfather, died a young man of an aneurysm. He died like a drink spills, leaving a young wife half-lived but fully-billed and with three kids to boot. Three, two and nine months, and one woman with one teacher's wages raising them, so is it any wonder that you came home for the holidays to her family?

In times like those a friendly face can turn hopelessness to coping.

She must have been lonely. And you must have known that. Maybe not when you were tiny, but difficult times mean growing up fast, even for the baby, the nine-month-old at the graveside. And maybe you felt lonely too, because you and her shared a life, till the end and the end.

That's something you did tell me, on our last Christmas, over and under drinks and technicolour treelight.

You were thinking, trying and failing to remember. And all that you could come up with of your father was this:

A taxi, black, and black clothes inside it on the way to the funeral.

Was that real or unreal, something you saw and kept before you were one? Or a picture plucked from a dream of the story, a detail you took from the telling and made more of, from the gleam of an eye inferring the face?

I don't know. But it was sad the way you told it to me. That your earliest memory of loss was your earliest memory. And your only of your father wasn't.

Those visits to our town were how you all met my mother. My father, you, and the oldest brother too. The three of them whether good or bad were definitely news and exciting with it.

So. Imagine the still cinema-ed mainstreet, still and Saturday quieted save for the sweet shop windowsill-sat riot of chat, mock combat, and other such messing collectively best known as

THE GANG. The yesteryouth, today's mothers and fathers, my ma among them, still living with theirs then. The ten and barelegged, the five and brylcreem-haired-headed mob, girls and boys both with more of mass to them than yob. These are not the bold kids, not the *sacred HEART do what you're TOLD or get a thump* kids, their worst for years yet'll be scrumping apples from the nuns' orchard. That is the all of their bête noirery, this first generation not threatened with the just closed reformatories.

They hang out outside the sweet shop and they don't buy sweets. Outside of Lent this is a neat demonstration of their not-childness, childish wants and toys both shelved. Not children but voyagers and they are discovering themselves, the place of each self amongst each of these others, the heart-racing excitement of skirts jeans or slacks lacking sister or brotherness. America meant less to Columbus than this does to this lot, these first flirtations with flirting, watched by their elders, who don't comment but do remember, and smilingly leave them to it because who's it hurting?

Now imagine the renown of being unknown to them, a dark-side-of-the-moon-rivalling mystery.

Imagine their arrival in those days, three lads London-raised but Cork-blooded and handsome. And my ma says of COURSE my da was, but you were AND then some.

Down the main road they come now with not a little swagger, watched by the gang with twenty and bored eyes, this threesome – a phrase then not yet pornified, or at least not to sixteen-year-olds.

Who was first to speak? Was it you? Was it my dad? Was it something smooth, was it something suave or its opposite? Did the speaker leave cursing his eejitry, or feeling tip-top about his Casanovish advances?

I don't know cos my ma doesn't, and she was the one there, but the one word she'll swear to is this:

Hello.

And from the facts it's clear that it was said in English accents.

Hello.

That's what she remembers, a word and the fact that you were handsome, so handsome.

And of course first glances aren't all there is to it, if it's the other brother you end up dancing with then no bother, dance away, sound.

But if it were glances, and glances alone, then you might not have been my uncle and father but rather, the other way round.

And even now, if you ask her, she'll say *Oh he was lovely.*

That's what she'll say, that *Oh, you were lovely.*

To a child, you were a one-man Christmas of a messer. You ripped the piss like a parent probably wished to but never did. Because a father or mother's is lawlove, a love with all of the lumps left in. The love that forbids sweets in fear of stumpteeth, of bedtimes and discipline, bathtimes and medicine, of handfuls of your hair full of freshly won grey ones.

Whereas you were as bold as we were, and you were allowed to swear.

You had not just a knack but a full-blown flair for teasing older women, a sly and behind-back kind of sleazy wit.

A woman'd pass us and you'd pass some remark like *Jesus the state of that aul bitch.*

And sometimes she'd turn and as-straightbackedly-as-eighty-can-manage inspect us, suspecting – and rightly so – that on some level our shite-breaking giggles were directed in her direction.

And you'd smile and wave like a portrait of the present, correct, and upright citizen, while delighting in our private not giving a shit and say something like:

Oh HELLO Mrs Shine.

Or, *LOVELY day Mrs Shoucroux, LOVELY day.*

It wasn't the not really meanness so much as the cursing amused us, we laughed as achingly much at the reverse of it, when you would make a Venus, Marilyn or Helen of her for the hell of it.

She'd see you, with your eyes blue and clear as a Scout's honour, not dreaming that you'd just leaned down and said:

GOD they're fine legs she's got on her.

RAVISHING. I'd marry her.

You'd have us inside out with the laughing without looking as though we were.

Or this, this one my younger brother's memory:

Of Patrick Street in the city, and the two of you between you moving a pane of glass. The twist being that it didn't exist, you were just playing and a pain in the collective ass of everyone who bought it.

Who did buy it?

Did the boys in their matching Adidas? Or gray and mohaired grannies dragging wheedling grandkids? Or partnerless business partners in I'm-still-single-breasted suits? Or frazzledly casual mammies and daddies on their kid-collecting routes? Who saw you there?

Does it even matter, who saw you, seeing as you didn't care.

Or if you did, that didn't stop you, or you wouldn't let that.

And my brother, who was and is as shy then as now, could briefly forget that fact and embrace the divine foolery, the flaunting of indifference like brazen jewellery.

We're not just in on the joke, we are it, and we love our own bizarrity.

I know now that you were a young man.

You weren't even forty, then, still as thin as you were at sixteen and face nearly as smooth. To a child, forty and eighty are equally removed so it follows they ajoin. I thought us the North and South Poles of the globe, white bears and flightless waterbirds, but you weren't even middle-aged, much less old.

If I were a bear, then you had barely reached the Tropic of Cancer, and if I were a penguin you'd yet to advance as far as Capricorn. Far enough from the cradle, maybe, but not yet headed graveward, much less dead, and you stayed as nifty with the mischief into your fifties.

You didn't make it to sixty.

I am glad, at least, I got to know you as an adult. If only for a short while.

My mam got close to four decades of you. About what my dad did, the margin after Dad's death like the length of your shared childhood, but still ten years behind your only brother still alive. Though he disappeared for years in the nineties, unfindable even after we consulted a psychic, unfindable even for the news my father had died. He found out and was found when someone he knew told him *Sorry for your loss*.

And he had to ask.

Which?

If we discount those years my mother was second only to yours. And there's no shame in that, you cared for your mother at her end like she for you at your start, left your job in London to mind her with her mind and body rechilding like you had once adulted. There was nothing and no one else like that: for you, at least.

I was just glad to be your friend, like they were, spend time with you, like they did. Glad we never faded from thievethick to once-a-year faces at Christmas, christenings or funerals. Glad I didn't grow up to find out you were racist, sexist, or uncomfortable with Jewish people. You were anti-Klan, anti-misogyny, anti-anti-Semitism. And you were not just not bad, but good craic and good at listening.

Had I had any secrets worth telling, I could have and would have told you.

But we still had loads to talk about for all that I lacked them.

And I am honoured, even though I never asked you, that you told me you were gay.

I hadn't known, and wouldn't have guessed.

My ma knew, as one of those who knew you best, but through my dad telling her, not you.

I wonder had you wanted to, had you last minute not managed for all that you planned to, or not managed to not have it taken from your hands like a small child's Easter egg. Or would you have rathered she never knew at all?

I don't think so, because you seemed so calm and unafraid in saying it to me.

No sense of occasion on that just one amongst many days like it, chatting in the house.

You said these words:

And by the way, I don't know why I never told you, but I'm gay.

And I said something wojus like:

Oh. That's great.

Not the best of all responses. But not the worst, or even bad enough that we didn't then have the first of all our talks about the whole thing. I don't know if my response was exactly what you wanted, but I hope at least you hadn't been thinking *please, NOT that* before I said that

For all that we talked, though, I've all the more questions.

You told me you were celibate, and would be for good, but whether that meant you never had or never again would, I don't know. If you had, I hope that you were glad you hadn't hadn't. And if you hadn't, I hope the thought of having had didn't hurt.

Once you said to me:

Maybe I'm just asexual

and it was almost like you expected me to tell you for once and for all and for sure if you were or if you weren't. And maybe if I had done then you'd've been relieved, but I didn't because I didn't and don't believe that you believed that, because who knew what you knew you wanted better than you did?

And that now reminds me of the diary that – while you were still alive – you allowed me to read part of, where you described seeing four young men by the river, and how in spite of the summer-proof and shivering cold of the water they stripped off to swim, hip and shoulderbonely angular as herons and how you, sitting lonely watching him jump in on top of him and him dunk him, were relieved not to desire them, or so you wrote, but still wrote about them.

And why would you notice desire's absence if, most or all of the time, it was absent? You wouldn't mark it unless it marked you, scored or scarred you as it passed through like some malign abscess that – try as you might to – you can't quite forget.

I think you wanted to be asexual because it's easier not to want something than want it and never get it.

Like Cyrano the musketeer, fearing to love someone who might not love him back.

And did you, like him, come to feel trapped in your celibacy?

Did you choose it freely or feel it was imposed on you because you were too old or not sufficiently beautiful? (Although you were, to those who knew you.)

Did you ever, like him, or the man who on a whim dragged a steamboat through the Amazon, wish you could go back on what you'd decided or done, but think it was too late and that the race couldn't be unrun, like it would be easier, now, to keep on than to not? Like the only thing more foolish than having started would be to stop?

I don't know.

You told me that clubs for gay people definitely weren't for you. But had you ever gone before, had you had an adventure and tried it? Were you knocking it having never even knocked on the door to that culture, let alone having then opened and gone inside it? Did you acknowledge the possibility to yourself before shelfing it and drawing that solemn and uncrossable line?

You were my age in London in 1979 when heaven opened and floods of the young and hotblooded flooded in biblically. Bang

began its third year with one and a rumble and the Embassy's
gays still outnumbered the straights, but were you there with
spirits and hair as high and down as the sky and the streets?

I don't know, but Georges or Capel in town make me think of
you, when boys as well-clubbed as sealpups bleedingly reel into
a crowdclot, as young and handsome as you first meeting my
mother outside a sweet shop.

As far as I know, you never saw the sweetness of this, the gasping
rarity and do-we-dare-ity of clasped hands clasped firmly or a
clandestine kiss. Never saw all of this happily packedness. Never
saw the not so youthful and youth alike in action, revolt, and
bright clothing. Would you have viewed them with envy? Or
sadness? Or anger? Or loathing? I don't know, but you'd never
had the heart to loathe anything and if you'd started then then it'd
surprise me.

Did you see yourself as out? Half out? Not in the whole world's
but your family at least's eyes? Was 'out' a term you recognised
as relevant to your life, and if it was was it a cross or a skeleton
or an elephant to be borne like Christ in the closet or in the
room? Was absolute outness a positive prospect or longed for
dream or did it seem like a Russian-dollishly endless labour,
outing yourself to these friends then those colleagues and
ultimately the neighbours, outing after outing with no end of out
in sight? You can travel till north souths or east wests or left
rights, but you never run out of outness to come out into.
There's seven billion someones living on this Earth so there's
always another someone you haven't told or who hasn't heard.

In our town, you could have been the first out man over thirty
but weren't, and I wonder was that for fear of hurting
friendships or family?

At your funeral I mentioned your sadnesses and was stopped
with an

I don't want to know

by one of your best and steadiest friends, and the madness of that
is that he must have known already to know he didn't want to.

You told me when you told my dad he told you:

go for it

but I don't know did your mother know. If she did and it
bothered her then did that bother you? If she didn't was it
because you couldn't tell her or because you didn't bother to?

Would she have used the word gay, in front of you in day-to-
week-to-month-to-year-to-sudden-several life as the pair of you
shared it? And if she did, did it scare you with its sneaking
relevance to a secret self, the shock of a sudden knock on a
forgotten-about-and-thought-solid hollowness?

Would she have used the word queer, with none of its modern
politics but a hint of a derision, nearly but not really hidden
under a false matter-of-factness like untrusting cash under an
ageing mattress?

Or would she, had you told her, have said she'd always known
and loved you none the less for it?

I don't know if she knew or cared, and there could be honour in
that breach, but her and your lifelong silence about it strikes me
as a kind of speech.

Did you not feel like it mattered if you had sworn off
entanglements, if after all soulsearching selfwrestling or pro and
con wrangling the only person you were going to share a life
with was her? You loved your mother like no one else, but did
giving her what you gave her feel like giving up on yourself?
Even a little, even a bit? Was doing what you did for her your
heartfelt wish or an accounting, a counting up of what it would
cost you, and if it was did it leave you feeling like you had lost
much, or just a little, or anything?

You had one brother left, with a history of disappearing and the
potential to again, or the potential to tarry and marry a nice lady
friend, but you weren't going to do either. Did you think:

it's only logical?

I think you probably thought that, if not always then sometimes.

By the time they were my age my parents were married, so in
the photos of the big day that show you all formally but

smilingly arrayed on the church steps in your best suits and dresses, you're a fair bit younger than I am now, your hair still long and unrulily tressing like a seventies disco idol's.

And my mother remembers you saying at some point something like:

I suppose I'll have to look after Mam now.

And neither she nor I really know why you thought that, let alone why you said it, let alone then and there on the day of their wedding, with the cake uncut and your mother not yet declining or even linefaced, let alone wrinkled or bentbacked.

And while you might have been right to think that, it would still be the length of your whole life up to that point before it ever came to be, and did it because you stencilled your life through that prophecy, never not conscious of that pencilled-in appointment on every day of every diary?

I don't know.

Another thing you told me that Christmas, our last one, was how much you missed my dad. You told me it was:

More than you'll ever know

and I never disagreed with or even doubted that, for all he was my father.

When I think of the two of you I picture the pictures you took as young men, stomachs sticking out in mock paunches with hands like pregnant women's pressed to your backs. A finite jest that's only funny to young men who don't think they'll ever themselves be fat.

You were, eventually, and I only mention it because I think you found it hard.

Your body was something you'd always taken pride in, its slim-and limberness, toned by swims and runs and dancing. You showed it off in suits you'd bought in your twenties that still fit beautifully, and the men who can claim that are few and far between.

Then, when your mother was getting worse, you couldn't do those things. Less moving or shaking, more late-night takeaways eaten exhaustedly after she'd gone asleep.

All you were lacking was more time, but you lacked it, and so the days got filled and the cartons got emptied, cleaned out, and stacked up, until you put away your suits and you started wearing tracksuits.

And it's not that a bit of fat is fundamentally awful, that's not what I'm saying, but losing something you've always been proud of is – always, but more so when already lonely and bereft – dismaying.

I wonder did you struggle with it, did you play the cruel game, where you win when you lose and you lose when you gain and you gain by doing nothing, or just not enough?

I hope but don't really think that you spared yourself the scanting, the *why not* excess of despair when it failed or grew too hard to stick with, or the growing reluctance to look down once the battle to suck it all in has been lost, decisively.

Of course we loved you anyway, if anything more than ever, but it seemed like you felt like you weren't the person you once were, but were stared at by strangers in windows and mirrors.

My dad got fatter too, but he never got fat because he never got a chance to, and both of you got older but neither of you got old.

So I can't help but wonder: would you have found getting older any easier with your older brother around if not to shoulder then at least acknowledge the mind and body's treasons? Would you have lived on into old age if he had?

I don't know.

I have one uncle left, the eldest of the three, as though our family tree is rotting from the bottom up in defiance of tradition. And I'm not saying I'd trade him for the two of you back, I love him for all I don't know him like I knew you, but I do wish that the two of you had lived as long as he did, as long as you could have done, as long as you should.

Wouldn't it be wonderful if the world were that fair, and our predecessors were and they did? If the living always became dead in the order they began to live, as strict as an alphabet or calendar.

But it is not, and never has been. Mothers bury sons, and fathers daughters, grandparents their children's children, then their children. Homes emptied by palindrome injustices, where firstborn not only lives longest, but buries the newest first.

I notice, sometimes, that the only one not lost to us is the only one who tried to be.

And I wonder would you have minded, out of modesty, that I've decided to talk to you and not my dad?

I do have questions I'd ask him, just like I'd ask you, if you, or he, or both of you had lived, because you were both younger brothers and you both died young. But my dad didn't choose to die and you did.

And the how or why of that having happened, trying to make sense or just less of a horrible mess of it, is a question as unanswerable as it is unignorable, so I hopelessly, here and now, in front of you, ask it.

Why?

I don't know.

I never will.

I kissed you in your coffin. I smelled the make-up. My brother, not even in the middle of his early twenties, handled your will and the attendant paperwork.

So in many ways my dad's death was much more mysterious.

Though you died alone you died at home, with family near, and my dad died far away in London amongst strangers.

He had a seizure in a restaurant, choked, and suffered brain damage.

I know his cause of death was 'cerebral hypoxia', but I don't know who was there or whether they looked shocked or didn't

notice or didn't care or if someone rushed to help him or if –
even if I wasn't a witness – it was witnessed by other children.

I don't know if it was a Chinese or Italian restaurant. So why
amn't I asking him those questions?

I saw far more of your latter, later, death, but for all I saw more
I understood less and was still left still wondering:

Why?

And it's not just that I don't know but that I don't think there's
an answer.

You used to go to hospital for weeks at a time, when your world
was rhyme and reasonless but all rock and hard place.

And you told me you were tormented in those times by your
gayness, but was that symptom or sickness?

Did it only hurt you when you already hurt, or was that always
there beneath a rictus as solitary as a fortress?

Were you tortured because you were ill, or were you ill because
you were tortured?

I don't know because I can't know because you couldn't tell me
because you couldn't speak.

You would call me, and I'd spend hours with the phone wedged
into my neck, my arm ridged from its worriedly-round-wound
cable. Just hearing you breathe, or trying to talk but unable to,
and all the while me feeling useless but close to you, or going to
visit and finding you weren't dressed because you'd forgotten
you were supposed to.

But that wasn't the first time that that had ever happened. In your
twenties your aunt once came in to find that you were naked in
her living room, or so my mother tells me, and that you didn't
say anything.

I wonder did she laugh, sincerely or surprisedly, or was she just
shocked, or appalled, or incensed? And what was going on on the
inside of your skull that that, to you, made any kind of sense?

I don't know, if anything, what you meant to say, but you spoke your anguish, your young and thinly spindling body a palely mute language when all others failed you.

Who, now, then, could deny you your suffering?

Were you, in your own mind, asking for help? Or declaring yourself as a victim, or an offering, or maybe even both, proffering the all of you as raw as a scald or an opened throat, to be done to or away with as anyone but you wished? Or was she interrupting some ancient moment, some throwing off of clothing like the first Olympians whose whole bodies were hands for taking hold of tasks? And if she was, and if you were like them, what was it you were trying to grasp?

I don't know, I wasn't there, and neither was my mother, so who could swear to the story's truth, after its passing and passing?

Other stories are ours: like how later, though you never had children yourself, you made children of my parents.

My brother and I would both sleep in my bed when they argued, or we'd pretend to at least, listening to these sudden strangers of adults like night-time beasts outside a tent, scared by their proximity and our limited understanding of what was going on and what the noises meant.

And we didn't know this, but they would sometimes lie awake too when you stayed with us, listening to you talk to no one, or yourself, or anyone who would listen, the two of them as scared and ununderstanding as their children.

And when that happened to me, finding you unclothed, for all that a body's just a body it was scary, feeling you were somewhere so removed that you'd forgotten all rules, like if not getting dressed was an option then what else might you do.

There's a weightlessness and a lack of aptness to the words *mental health*, they don't capture the terror I felt those times when you were a stranger to yourself.

The night you died you tried to get admitted to the hospital, but were refused because you lacked a doctor's note and name.

The taxi driver who drove you there and back home afterward was the last person who saw you.

This is where the asking begins and ends.

It is or was your house, your apartment, at least, and maybe home. You only ever lived alone in it and I don't know if it felt like one.

It can't have in comparison with your mother's on the main street, whose walls were the bookends of your child-and-then-adulthood. Someone else lives there now, which bothers me like it bothered you, after and before her and your deaths.

After she was gone you stayed with us as often as you stayed in this new apartment, and we'd started to do up the spare room as your room. You went before we finished, and it was a strange decision we then had to make: continue, leave it in between, or go back.

I sometimes wonder what else you left like that, a paused video that seesaws endlessly from just-gone frame to just-to-come frame, faces and limbs through limbs and faces in neither chimeras as grotesque as they are aimless.

One thing I know about: when your mother died, I received a bequeathment I never even wanted, and only because her will – which left you everything – was made too late in her life to be valid.

Her lawyer, while fighting for it, in a cack-handed attempt at unneeded comfort, told me:

Don't worry, he'll leave it to you when he dies!

Which might be why you named my just-about-not-a-baby brother as your executor, rather than have her again. You probably thought he'd be older when the time came.

I found that cheque when we were cleaning your apartment, you'd never even cashed it.

I thought that was strange, but this part's the important part.

It is four days since the burial, and I'm in the room you slept in, which I've tiptoe crept into although I know there's no one

I could possibly wake. What matter if it makes sense, but noise feels wrong, to put the foot down uncarefully as garish as song.

I'm not actually upset, the act feels remote from this not-remotely-nightmarish place: fewer signs of its having happened than of you having lived here. I will always have more memories of other visits than this one, years of the easy ones and only then the harder, which were always so much fewer even if, now, they loom larger in the light of your death.

I didn't look at the fireplace with its shelf where your note was, not could not, did not, and I passed over the point itself without thinking.

I just go to your bedroom, see the bed with mussed-up bedcovers and the window, dust-covered, and the dust itself carved into the opposite of a finger-painting.

CLAIRE *draws crosses in the air with a fingertip.*

You drew with what's not there. Dust the ground and the figure is absence, making this, in a sense, a portrait of the artist. I see disconnected bits of the field that sits beyond it, brindle and brindle skies and cows at their fodder. I think: this image isn't, it's just the breaking up of another into this graveyard of crosses, and each cross a question.

When did you do this?

A week, a month, a year ago?

And what were you thinking?

Was it in health or sickness?

An idle moment, or a devout, or a diverted?

Or holed up here and holding still, not because it helps, but for fear you might feel worse yet than you've yet managed to feel?

Like it was when you would call me?

I do not – and never will – know. You were all of those sometimes.

Your earliest memory was of loss, but mine is of you.

First is the cold and its colour, like washed-out dye, a grey seaside sky and the sand under its vagueness.

You are swimming, you're out past the point where the waves break and no signs of stopping.

Me and my brother wrapped in towels and, rapt, watch your bluecapped head bobbing onward. It's all we can see of you, seen through my own seatangled hair like a veil. And Gran's now paused in her between-toe towelling of us to watch you as well, as you push like a pin into a wall through the swells but outward, not in. Always outward. Away from the certain rise of land to the horizon's lack:

And we're confused, suddenly, because Gran says:

Mother of God oh Mother of God, he's not going to come back.

And I don't understand why she'd say something like that, because you will.

And you did.

And we watched that wee smudge of a head as it slid slowly shoreward.

No one budged until it seemed like a sure thing, you close enough if not to put a foot down now then soon, soon, soon.

Your blue amongst the white caps, whole and breaking, and up amongst the dunes your family aching for the moment when you rise up, spat out, safe.

And you did, and you were, and you ran the length of the beach to us, laughing.

www.nickhernbooks.co.uk

facebook.com/nickhernbooks

twitter.com/nickhernbooks